Internet Sex Work

Teela Sanders · Jane Scoular
Rosie Campbell · Jane Pitcher
Stewart Cunningham

Internet Sex Work

Beyond the Gaze

Teela Sanders
University of Leicester
Leicester, UK

Jane Scoular
University of Strathclyde
Glasgow, UK

Rosie Campbell
University of Leicester
Leicester, UK

Jane Pitcher
University of Strathclyde
Glasgow, UK

Stewart Cunningham
University of Strathclyde
Glasgow, UK

ISBN 978-3-319-65629-8   ISBN 978-3-319-65630-4 (eBook)
https://doi.org/10.1007/978-3-319-65630-4

Library of Congress Control Number: 2017952824

© The Editor(s) (if applicable) and The Author(s) 2018
This work is subject to copyright. All rights are solely and exclusively licensed by the Publisher, whether the whole or part of the material is concerned, specifically the rights of translation, reprinting, reuse of illustrations, recitation, broadcasting, reproduction on microfilms or in any other physical way, and transmission or information storage and retrieval, electronic adaptation, computer software, or by similar or dissimilar methodology now known or hereafter developed.
The use of general descriptive names, registered names, trademarks, service marks, etc. in this publication does not imply, even in the absence of a specific statement, that such names are exempt from the relevant protective laws and regulations and therefore free for general use.
The publisher, the authors and the editors are safe to assume that the advice and information in this book are believed to be true and accurate at the date of publication. Neither the publisher nor the authors or the editors give a warranty, express or implied, with respect to the material contained herein or for any errors or omissions that may have been made. The publisher remains neutral with regard to jurisdictional claims in published maps and institutional affiliations.

Cover illustration: Pattern adapted from an Indian cotton print produced in the 19th century

Printed on acid-free paper

This Palgrave Macmillan imprint is published by Springer Nature
The registered company is Springer International Publishing AG
The registered company address is: Gewerbestrasse 11, 6330 Cham, Switzerland

Acknowledgements

The people and organisations who have helped the Beyond the Gaze research project have made it feel like a network of many across virtual and physical spaces. It's impossible to acknowledge and name them all, not just because of the number of people who have assisted but also due to the ethics and sensitivities of our research, particularly the need to protect confidentiality and anonymity. We thank all those working in the sex industry who have supported the research in a myriad of ways including taking part in interviews, the survey, promoting and championing the research and advising us. This includes especially sex workers, but also their customers, sex worker and customer forums, those working in adult service-related ITC, advertising and marketing, academic and legal experts, sex worker rights organisations and sex work projects. We may not be able to name you, but you know who you are and we are indebted. The same goes to the police forces who contributed to interviews, the individual officers who took part, the NPCC lead on sex work and their staff officers. The Economic and Social Research Council (ES/M007324/2) provided the funding which enabled BtG to happen. Thanks, in the analysis stage, to Dr. Stephen Corson at the University of Strathclyde and Emily Sherman at the University of Leicester. Thanks especially are extended to our community co-researchers within the BtG team and to our formal partners: National Ugly Mugs, Basis Sex Work Project and SAAFE.

Contents

1 Introduction: Technology, Social Change and Commercial Sex Online — 1

2 The Digital Sexual Commerce Landscape — 23

3 Characteristics and Working Practices of Online Sex Workers — 55

4 Crimes and Safety in the Online Sex Industry — 87

5 Policing Online Sex Markets — 121

6 Conclusion: Key Messages — 153

Appendix: Data Sample Overview — 165

Index — 177

List of Figures

Fig. 2.1	Online spaces sex workers use for support and information	41
Fig. 3.1	Respondents' age group by gender. $N = 641$	59
Fig. 3.2	Types of work undertaken. $N = 641$	66
Fig. 3.3	Average hours worked per week. $N = 641$	70
Fig. 3.4	To what extent do you agree or disagree with the following statements about the use of the Internet and digital technologies for your work? $N = 641$	76
Fig. 4.1	Internet's role in safety strategies. $N = 641$	96
Fig. 4.2	Enhancing safety at work. $N = 641$. Multiple response question, so percentages add up to more than 100	99
Fig. 4.3	Steps to protect identity online	112

List of Tables

Table 3.1 Average gross annual income from sex work
          (before any deductions including taxes)   71
Table 4.1 Have you experienced any of the following crimes
          or incidents in the past 5 years and/or past 12 months
          in your current sex work job?   89

1

Introduction: Technology, Social Change and Commercial Sex Online

Abstract Technology, particularly digital communication, has had a profound impact on how we organise our lives, conduct our relationships and the transactions of commerce and retail (van Dijk in The network society, Sage, London, 1991/2012). Sex work is part of this digitally networked society. Increasingly sex is sold via the internet. Most sex workers and their customers make contact using technology (phone, email, text, websites) to facilitate in-person services and arrange offline encounters, but equally important the digital revolution has created a medium through which sexual services are sold only online through indirect contact. This introductory chapter has four functions: (1) to provide a short overview of the literature in relation to commercial sex and digital changes; (2) to introduce the project *Beyond the Gaze: Working Practices, Safety and Regulation of Internet based sex work* and the key messages relayed in the book; (3) to specifically outline the methodologies used to gather the data; (4) to contextualise what direct and indirect sex work online actually involve.

Keywords Digital revolution · Networked society · Sex markets
Direct/indirect sex work · Participatory action research · Limitations of
the study · Datasets · Netreach · Good practice guidelines
National ugly mugs

This introduction has four functions: (1) to provide a short overview of the literature in relation to commerce sex and digital changes; (2) to introduce the project *Beyond the Gaze: Working Practices, Safety and Regulation of Internet based sex work* and the key messages relayed in the book; (3) to specifically outline the methodologies used to gather the data; and (4) to contextualise what direct and indirect sex work online actually involve.

Technology, particularly digital communication, has had a profound impact on how we organise our lives, conduct our relationships and the transactions of commerce and retail (van Dijk 1991/2012). These technological developments have had a significant impact on forms of social organisation and the spatial distribution of human activities, with new social structures emerging which Castells (2000) has termed the 'network society'. Sex work is part of this digitally networked society. Increasingly, sex is sold via the Internet. Most sex workers and their customers make contact using technology (phone, email, text and websites) to facilitate in-person services and arrange offline encounters, but equally important, the digital revolution has created a medium through which sexual services are sold only online through indirect contact. Social changes in society have transformed the sex industry in the twenty-first century. Brents and Hausbeck (2010) have commented on the way in which cultural and economic changes in Western societies have influenced sexual attitudes and practices, as well as the context in which sex is sold. Brents and Sanders (2010) observe that these trends have contributed to a mainstreaming of the sex industry in the West, as economic business strategies are mirrored by sex businesses, gaining them legitimacy and reputation. Nonetheless, 'the acceptability of the sex industry is as much about social class, race and ethnicity as it is about liberal attitudes toward sexuality' (Brents and Hausbeck 2010, p. 16). As Bernstein (2007) notes, there has been an increasing 'privatisation' of the sex industry, as sex workers move from street-based to indoor work. A combination of changes; in sexual attitudes, mainstreaming of the sex industry and a move to private commercial sex (as opposed to public and visible) are contemporary themes which underpin and inform the move to digitally facilitated commercial sex.

The development of Internet-enabled sex work must be situated in the context of technological and structural transformations in the global economy. For instance, there continues to be a 'digital divide' between those who do or do not have access to Internet-based technologies (Min 2010). This divide also translates into sex work, where although independent sex workers tend to have an online profile and often their own website, those working in other sectors such as massage parlours do not necessarily have Internet access (Pitcher 2014). Further, there are disparities between groups in relation to cultural capital, where individuals do not have the capacity and resources to engage in the digital economy in the same way as those with access to resources. One such group are migrant sex workers who may be disadvantaged, hindered by language capabilities and citizenship status and less able than others control digital interfaces. Whilst there is some evidence to suggest that migrant workers are becoming dominant in certain indoor UK sex markets sectors (Association of Chief Police Officers 2010) or geographical areas (see Chap. 2) their online presence is not evident in the same numbers, particularly when scanning independent escort websites.

Internet-based sex markets have become pervasive (Sanders 2005a, b, 2008), facilitated by computer-mediated communication through email, chat rooms, social media forums and web-based advertising. As Ray (2007) and others have noted, the Internet has had a substantial impact on the way in which independent sex workers, as well as escort agencies and sometimes massage parlours, advertise their services. Studies on the way in which the Internet is used for commercial sexual transactions and advertising by sex workers show that this has not only changed how sex workers and clients communicate with one another but also their social relationships, with the development of 'cyber communities' of both sex workers and customers (Sharp and Earle 2003; Sanders 2005b; Walby 2012; Pitcher 2015a). As with other industries, the Internet has also facilitated not only advertising of sexual services but also provided the opportunity for customers to review services of individual providers, which has become an important aspect of online marketing (Lee-Gonyea et al. 2009; Pettinger 2011).

It is impossible to identify the very precise time when sex workers began to move online but the first ever sex work-related website was reportedly launched in 1994 by a Seattle-based escort agency (Hughes 2004). Writing back in 2003, Sharp and Earle note that 'any Internet search will reveal, there are literally tens of thousands of websites dedicated, in one way or another, to prostitution, and this number is increasing all the time' (Sharp and Earle 2003, p. 37). Sharp and Earle's observation is reflected in our research findings, which show that most of the major market leading platforms in the UK opened their websites in the early to mid 2000s. Platform 1, for example, launched their first site in 2003 using a 'co.uk' domain address moving over to their existing '.com' version in 2005. Several of the other platform owners that we interviewed identified a similar timeline (early to mid 2000s) for the development of their websites. Aimed at the male gay market, the owner of Platform 17 launched in 2002 and the owners of Platforms 16 and 44 both said they started their sites about ten years ago, which at the time of interview would indicate a starting time of around 2006. It is apparent from several studies (e.g. Sharp and Earle 2003; Cunningham and Kendall 2011; Pitcher 2015b) that Internet-based sex work is a growing and developing sector in the UK and internationally. There has been no comprehensive research attempting to quantify this growth, although certain studies (e.g. Import.io 2014; Pitcher 2014; Smith and Kingston 2015) have undertaken small-scale analyses of particular websites advertising sexual services to present estimates of different groups of sex workers advertising online.

Our primary aims for the book are as follows:

1. Chapter 2 establishes the landscape of Internet-based sex work and specifically the micro-practices of sex work online, new sex markets and how the markets are organised and operate. We focus specifically on how new technologies have reshaped and reoriented the sex markets examining the features that have emerged in online (indirect) sex work such as webcamming. We learn more about how sex workers are owning and using digital spaces for their own business as well as to politically organise and engage.

2. Chapter 3 explores the profile and characteristics of sex workers who completed our survey across the gender spectrum who sell sex that is providing new information about how commercial sex is structured and organised.
3. Chapter 4 examines the new forms of crimes facilitated by the online environment such as doxing, misuse of images, persistent harassment as well as everyday privacy concerns. To counteract that, we explore the detailed data from 62 interviews with sex workers which consider the new style safety strategies which merge with more 'old school' measures for keeping safe.
4. In Chap. 5, we ask about the role of the police in Internet-based sex work. Given the Internet is largely self-regulating, we ask how does self-regulation of sex work operate? Who are the actors, what are norms, how can these be strengthened and what is the relationship between self-regulation and formal policing? We want to question whether it is realistic for policing to include Internet-based sex work, and the ways in which safety and support can be developed for this hidden yet sizeable community.
5. In the conclusion, we draw out some of the key messages that we have learnt from this project to assess the impact that digital technologies have on work, safety, crimes and policing.

Methodologies, Collaborations and Partnerships

Our underlining principles were driven by a participatory action research approach, particularly with sex workers, which would form the ways in which the project developed. We involved sex workers in several ways: (1) as paid co-researchers on the project; (2) through an advisory board who would act as sounding points for various methodological decisions throughout the design and piloting phases, points of analysis, guidance on safety resources and good practice guidelines; and involvement in dissemination activities; and (3) through a participatory film to synthesise the findings for a lay audience.

Given the project was underpinned by PAR, we had a methodological approach on which to then design our project. We considered that a mixed methods approach, drawing on the traditions of qualitative and quantitative data collection methods, would best suit the far-reaching and diverse aims of the project. Qualitative methods, namely, through in-depth semi-structured interviews, would enable detailed information to be drawn out from sex workers, key informants in the online businesses and the police, providing space to talk at length about a vast range of issues. Given the sensitive nature of the sample population and the absolute need for strict ethical protocols, systems of confidentiality and discretion, the interviews were carefully designed tools that mapped onto the groups we wanted to recruit.

Quantitative survey methods were also appropriate as we wanted to find out more information about the trends and patterns of behaviour from sex workers and their customers. We were also aware that researchers in this field have often shied away from traditional positivist notions of quantitative methods, particularly given the significant wealth of data and understanding produced from ethnographic and talking-based methods (Sanders 2006). Yet given the boom in sex work research that has taken place in the past decade, the lack of innovation in merging methods and approaches through deeply ethical processes has meant that the number work has not been done. This has resulted in a lack of information to bring to the table, particularly in the context of policy and parliamentary arenas where numbers talk, resulting in policy often based on a very partial understanding of the sex industry. We designed a set of tools which would enable us to both capture the rich detail of everyday lives but equally in the broader contexts of trends and patterns relating to sexual labour, sexual consumption and the organisation of the sex industry online. The tools were developed with our co-researchers from the sex work community in addition to our advisory group. The tools were checked for relevance, wording and appropriate language, whether questions would help elucidate the information sought, and importantly for recruitment strategies.

Interviews with Sex Workers

Semi-structured interviews were deployed to gather qualitative data about online sex workers experiences and views. This covered six broad topics: reasons for sex working; use of Internet for sex work;

presenting the self online and intimacy; safety; privacy and regulation; and support for sex workers. Questions for those who also did webcamming included relationships with clients; providing a service; and privacy and safety. All people taking part in interviews also completed two forms; first, a 'Sex Worker Participant Basic Information Sheet' which collected quantitative data about key socio-demographic variables, and second, participants completed a form about their job characteristics in terms of how long, where, what markets, hours of pay, rates of pay and other work. Participants were recompensed £20 for their time. Interviews were carried out between November 2015 and October 2016. Four researchers conducted 62 interviews through different mediums: $n = 32$ were telephone interviews, $n = 14$ were carried out face-to-face, $n = 2$ used WhatsApp, $n = 9$ were Skype video interviews and $n = 5$ were Skype phone calls. These options enabled the participant to choose what mode of contact they preferred. Our concern was to obtain a sample of sex workers diverse in terms of sex work jobs they had, geography (region/home nation-based) and gender identity. After initial call outs to sex workers, the characteristics of the sample were monitored carefully, and specific call outs were issued stressing participation was required from particular cohorts of sex workers, for example, male sex workers, trans sex workers and migrant sex workers; specific calls were made to webcammers to ensure people in that specific job role were represented in the sample. The final sample demographics are available in the Appendix.

Survey with Sex Workers

In devising the survey, we replicated core questions on qualifications, age and ethnic categories from the Office for National Statistics guidance (2015). In relation to job satisfaction, we included a general question which is similar to that in other tools such as the European Working Conditions Survey. In the piloting stage, we received responses from ten sex workers (seven female and three male) in different sectors, including independent/agency sex work, BDSM, sexual massage and camming. The survey questionnaire was revised to consider comments from the pilot stage, which related to issues such as clarification or suggested changes to question wording, the relevance or appropriateness of specific questions or precoded categories and suggestions for additional categories in checklists.

Given that there is no comprehensive sampling frame for sex workers in different sectors working via the Internet (Shaver 2005), and that this remains a hidden group, we were not able to obtain a simple random sample. We are conscious this sampling method may lead to some self-selection bias and that certain groups of sex workers may not have seen the invitation to participate, or have been reluctant to take part in a formal survey and thus we may not have reached more hidden populations of people working in the UK sex industry. Nonetheless, when comparing our findings with those of other studies of independent internet-based sex workers, we may be reasonably confident that our survey sample represents a broad cross-section, in terms of factors such as gender, age, working sector and geographical diversity, of individuals working independently of their own volition in online sex work. In order to reach the maximum number of potential respondents, we sent out an invitation to take part in the survey, with a link, through a number of different sources where female, male and transgender sex workers advertise or provide their services. The survey commenced on 7th November 2016. By the end of 2016, the survey had been promoted on 15 advertising websites, Beyond the Gaze's own website, on social media (Twitter and Facebook), through sex work projects' contacts and by snowballing methods. The survey closed on 23rd January 2017, with 652 completed responses and 6 partial responses, which were removed prior to analysis. A further 11 respondents neither lived nor worked in the UK, and these were also removed from the data set, leaving a final total of 641 respondents living and/or working in the UK. A profile of respondents is shown in the Appendix.

Recruitment Online

Our recruitment methods for sex worker interviews and the two surveys (sex workers and customers) were based on a range of methods, but mostly facilitated through web platforms where sex workers advertise. Much time was spent building up research relationships with the key platforms so the recruitment process could reach the broadest range of respondents working in the UK. We are confident that no other study in the UK has worked with as many platforms, or achieved similar levels of access to private spaces on the closed website. We were able to achieve this through the support of key allies in the sex industry and those who introduced us to business owners. The project was privileged to have direct support from key platforms who displayed advertising banners promoting the surveys and call for interviewees. We also utilised social media activity as a recruitment method, through our Twitter site and also enjoyed considerable exposure via co-researchers postings and 'tweets' from sex workers who championed the research. Individuals also provided soundbite interviews for social media dispersal and went on the record clarifying our bona fide status as a research group.

Police and Web Platform Interviews

Two interview guides were designed for stakeholders, one for police and a second for IT, web platform, marketing and other online services representatives. We carried out a total of 35 interviews with police representatives, through these we interviewed a total of 56 police officers (plus $n = 2$ local authority representatives located in a multi-agency team with police) from $n = 16$ force areas across Scotland, Northern Ireland, Wales and England (with representation from all English regions including North West, North East, Midlands, Yorkshire and Humber, North East, East of England, South West, London and the South East). Our sample had good representation geographically, including all UK nations and regions and representing different policies and laws on sex work.

To gain further insight into the commercial and business aspect of the digital landscape, 11 interviews were carried out with 12 individuals (one joint interview) representing IT, web platform and marketing stakeholders. Amongst those interviewed were webmasters for advertising platforms, owners of advertising platforms/hook-up apps/porn site, representatives from a profile building service used by cam models and web designers specialising in design for sex workers. The sample included representatives from market lead advertising sites in the UK for female, male and transgender sex workers as well as smaller platforms.

Parameters and Limitations of the Study

There are limitations with this study, partly reflecting the specific research questions, but also methodological barriers researching the sex industry. In terms of the parameters of the study, we made a clear and conscious decision not to include modern slavery as an area of research, given the very specific relationship between commercial sex trafficking and organised crime through the Internet (see the special issue by Lerum and Brents 2016; Thakor and Boyd 2013). Researching how modern slavery and commercial sexual exploitation is facilitated through the Internet would have required specific partners (namely, police crime analysts) who have access to highly confidential information and work across the 'dark net', for instance (see ACPO 2010). Including modern slavery would have necessitated a different methodological approach and framework and one we felt could not be combined with the current broader questions we had about how digital technologies had changed the sex industry.

One of our main limitations is the lack of migrant sex worker representation in the study. In 2015 when BtG research commenced, many outreach and support projects throughout the UK who participated in the BtG and NUM practitioners group reported significant portions of migrant sex workers present in their local sex markets with Eastern Europe being the main area of origin and Romanians forming the largest migrant group amongst cis female sex workers. Those who carried out netreach reported significant proportions of migrants advertising in certain online spaces, they also found that this group was the hardest to make contact with, acknowledging a range of additional barriers to service access and support networks faced by migrants (Platt et al. 2011). Migrant people constituted 15% of people who took part in our survey and 16% of our interviewees. This is below the level of migrant sex workers found in indoor sectors in existing research.

Transparency is crucial for researchers and we need to reflect on why this is the case. Were migrants who work online in direct and indirect services under-represented in our study? Were they less likely to be working in the online sector than their UK counterparts? Or were they working in different ways? We think the former and latter could both be the case. There are several reasons why migrants are likely to be under-represented in this study; our promotional materials and the survey were not available in any languages other than English. Research has shown migrant sex workers, particularly those without papers who are of irregular or illegal status, are suspicious and wary of 'authorities' (Mai 2009)—this can include researchers from universities. Research and practice work with migrants in the UK sex industry has highlighted the importance of community development work, participatory action research and peer involvement models for effectively engaging sex worker generally and migrants specifically. We adopted a PAR approach but despite reaching out in adverts and via our networks for community co-researchers from migrant communities, none applied and timescales worked against a deeper ethnographic and community development approach which could be more effective in involving migrants. Clearly, further dedicated research is needed to be carried out with migrants working in the UK online sex industry to further explore migrants experiences of this sector, and this is particularly pressing with migrant sex workers often constructed in media and policy discourses in a reductionist manner as purely victims of modern slavery and trafficking.

Our Data—Bringing Together the Strands

Individual components of the study were as follows:

- Online survey of 641 sex workers based in and/or working in the UK, who use the Internet in their work;

- Semi-structured interviews with 62 sex workers of all genders who use the Internet for their work: 42 cis[1] females, 16 cis males and 4 trans workers;
- Semi-structured interviews with 56 police officers across 16 forces in England, Wales, Scotland and Northern Ireland;
- Twelve individuals representing IT, web platform and marketing stakeholders;
- Online survey of 1323 customers of sex workers using the Internet;
- Online survey of 49 projects providing support to online sex workers; and
- Desk research to map online spaces where sex workers market and/or provide services.

Partnerships

National Ugly Mugs (NUM) were our main partners in the research, as the leading NGO focused on sex worker safety in the UK. NUM is a nationally recognised, multi-award winning project founded in 2012. It aims to provide greater access to justice and protection for sex workers. Individual sex workers, organisations who work with sex workers, sex work establishments and online forums can sign up to NUM's third party reporting and alert scheme. NUM has promoted all aspects of BtG to its members, supported the development of safety information for online sex workers and helped establish the 'practitioners group'. This is a group of practitioners from projects delivering support services to sex workers in different areas of the UK; members of this group have supported BtG and informed the production of good practice guidance for working with online sex workers (which are discussed in the following text).

The National Police Chief Council's lead for prostitution and their staff officers have supported BtG, advising on and facilitating contact with police forces, distributing research briefings to forces across England and Wales (and to contacts in the devolved nations) and supporting final year knowledge sharing events. The latter enabling findings from BtG to be shared and discussed with single points of contacts for prostitution and other officers with leading strategic roles related to prostitution throughout forces.

Basis Yorkshire is an award winning third sector charity which works with cis female and transgender women working in all sectors of the sex industry offering information, safety and support through its specialist service 'Basis Sex Work Project'. Since the commencement of 'Beyond the Gaze', the Research and Netreach Officer has worked with staff and volunteer members of Basis Sex Work Project to develop netreach provisions for online sex workers in Leeds, learning from which has been shared via the BtG and NUM 'practitioners group'.

SAAFE (support and advice for sex workers) is a website and forum established over a decade ago by UK-based independent sex workers, providing an online space where sex workers can network and get advice and support from other sex workers. SAAFE advised on a number of elements of the project (e.g. survey design) and have provided a space on the forum to advertise for specific including community researcher recruitment, interview and survey participation, and findings dissemination have been promoted.

Practical Activities: Netreach, Resources and Networks

Our project had some very specific practical and policy focused aims achieved through the following activities:

1. From the commencement of BtG, the Research and Netreach Officer has worked with Basis Sex Work Project to enhance and expand netreach provisions within the project utilising a participatory approach. This has led to a weekly netreach service for sex workers in Leeds integrated into Basis, with the promotion of the information, advice and support available to workers in online sectors across a range of online forums, platforms and social media used by sex workers. It has also included the introduction of a live chat information and advice facility for sex workers.

2. The BtG and NUM 'practitioners group' has provided a forum where projects can share their experiences of providing services for online sex workers, including netreach provisions, practice challenges and share good practice. The Research and Netreach Officer has facilitated this group and encouraged practitioner networking. This has led to several organisations introducing new initiatives or changing practice to better meet the needs of Internet-enabled sex workers.
3. Bespoke findings briefings for the police and policymakers, and knowledge share and training events for police officers from a range of police forces. With the support of the National Police Chief Councils lead on sex work, briefings and other activities have been able to be targeted at key offices with operational or strategic responsibilities for sex work and related areas of policing across the UK. These activities have contributed to increasing police knowledge about the online sex work sector and particularly current crime issues affecting workers in the online sector and the barriers experienced in relation to reporting work-related crime.
4. *'Good practice guidance for working with online sex workers'* has been co-produced with NUM, available through the NUM and BtG websites. This gives practical information about a range of aspect of service development and delivery, for example, needs assessment, sex worker involvement, models of netreach, migrant sex worker's needs, ethical considerations and netreach worker skills. The guidance provides a legacy from the project, it is hoped this guidance resource will inform the development of quality, needs-based ethically delivered services for sex workers which will have benefits for sex workers, projects and other health and social care providers who have a role in service provision for sex workers.
5. *'Specialist online safety information resource for internet based sex workers'*. This is available on the BtG and NUM's websites and has been informed by the extensive data collected by BtG in which online sex workers have shared their safety strategies. Further 'expert by experience' input was ensured with online sex workers taking a lead in the working group who produced the safety information.

Different Forms of Internet-Enabled Sex Work

We use the term Internet-based sex work in our research to describe the use of the Internet and communication technologies to facilitate, in some way, commercial sex transactions. We draw a clear distinction between direct in-person and indirect sex work in our definition of Internet-based sex workers, which is:

> Sex workers based on their own, or in collectives, or working through an agency, who use the internet to market or sell sexual services either directly through in-person services (i.e. interacting with clients in person e.g. escorting, erotic massage, BDSM) or through online indirect services (i.e. interacting with clients online e.g. web camming).

Direct Internet-based or enabled sex work refers to commercial sex activities that take place in-person between the sex worker and customer, but that are advertised and arranged online, taking the form of escorting, as well as the provision of BDSM services and sexual massage. Indirect Internet-enabled sex work refers to activities that are both facilitated and take place in an online or virtual environment; examples include webcamming, instant message and phone sex chat. In webcamming, the models (also known as performers) provide shows, often but not always including nudity or sexual content, in front of their webcams, which are then streamed to customers watching on their own personal devices (computers/tablets/phones).

Instant messaging or SMS Chat involves sex workers providing a text chat service to customers. It operates like text messaging where the sex worker and customer communicate via typed messages on their personal devices. Some adult platforms facilitate instant messaging and allow the sex worker and customer to receive messages from each other without having to share any contact information as the messages are sent through a facility on the website. Instant messaging is charged by the messages received from the sex worker, and there are character limits per message. Prices vary on different platforms. In our interviews, some sex workers spoke of companies who paid them 8p for every text message they sent to a client. On Platform 1, the customer pays 1 credit

(£1) to start a text conversation and then 0.5 credit (50p) for every subsequent message received from the sex worker. The sex worker will receive approximately 70% of this income.

Phone sex chat is not an innovation of the digital age but we classify it as a form of indirect Internet-enabled sex work because it has also evolved with technological innovations. Jill (53), who had been doing phone sex chat as part of her sex work repertoire over a 15-year period describes some of the changes the Internet brought to the way she does phone sex work:

> Yeah, but they've integrated [the phone sex chat service] with the internet. So, what happens is, you can go and log on—and you don't have to do that through your phone, you can do that through the internet—and then you just transfer the calls through. Now, also, [the phone sex chat company] allow you to use mobile, which they never let you do before. It was always a fixed landline.

Another key form of indirect sex work that we observed was the growth in individual sex workers creating and selling their own sexual content (pictures and videos) online. Many of our interview participants had private photograph galleries online and would sell access to clients on escort advertising platforms or via apps like Snapchat (an instant messaging phone application). Many also created video clips of themselves, which they would sell on to clients on specialist content delivery platforms (described in Chap. 2). Cara (19), a webcammer, describes the benefits of creating and selling content online:

> If you've got enough videos, there's quite a lot of money in it for you … I thought, I don't know, camming takes effort whereas videos, once they're there, it's kind of making the money for you.

Anne (25), another webcammer, sells access to her Snapchat account by way of a monthly subscription, which enables clients to access the content she posts. She described how she posted '*random stuff throughout the day, like hello, or if I see something cute I'll post it or whatever*' as well as more sexual content:

A lot of the times if I am actually making an effort to look nice I will send them pictures of the, you know, the process, like, this is me without makeup, this is me naked, I'm having a shower, that sort of stuff.

Anne's use of Snapchat is an example of the creativity and entrepreneurship that flourishes in all forms of online businesses, including online sex work. The BtG research shows that sex workers, albeit to varying degrees, have embraced both the creative potential and income generating opportunities provided by new forms of digital communication and online connectivity.

Crossover Between Direct and Indirect Sex Work

A crucial finding from our research is the significant level of crossover amongst Internet-based sex workers into different forms of online sex work. The BtG survey findings show that only 16% ($n = 41$) of the respondents who worked as webcammers did so exclusively, which accords with our findings from the interviews. The webcammers in our survey undertook other forms of indirect sex work, with almost 60% ($n = 152$) offering phone sex chat services, 23% ($n = 58$) adult film work and 21% ($n = 52$) modelling, which includes making and selling self-made videos online. Also, 50% ($n = 127$) of the webcammers offered direct services as independent escorts, and 38% ($n = 96$) did BDSM work. It was much more common for independent escorts to undertake no other form of online sex work, which applied to 41% ($n = 196$) of independent escorts who participated in our survey. That still means, however, that most independent escorts did undertake some other form of sex work with 27% ($n = 127$) offering webcamming and 23% ($n = 111$) phone sex chat.

Some sex workers started out offering direct services and then supplemented this with indirect work online. It was common in qualitative interviews for sex workers who predominantly offered in-person escorting/BDSM/massage work to note that they used indirect services such as private galleries, or camming/phone/instant message services to earn money to pay for their escort advertising. As Alice (46, independent sex worker providing other services) notes, when discussing the upgrades for escort advertising she pays for on Platform 1, *'they cost me no money at all … the nude pictures that I put on my private gallery pay for everything'*. For Alice, offering direct services (escorting) was her main form of business, and indirect services (private photo galleries) were offered to facilitate the provision of direct services.

A move in the other direction was also apparent amongst some of our interviewees who initially planned only to offer indirect work, e.g. camming, and then moved into providing direct services, sometimes after requests from clients.

> Well, I was, I originally intended to be a webcammer only. So when I first signed up to Platform 1, I was like, right, I'm just gonna webcam. Escorting did not come into my mind (laughs) at all. It wasn't until I set up a profile and I put webcamming in it, and then I went to bed and then I woke up the next morning and I don't think I thought I was really gonna go through with it, but then I woke up the next morning and I had a lot of emails from clients, but they did not want to webcam with me (laughs). And that's how I ended up escorting. (Anna, 23, independent sex worker also a webcam worker)

The sharp entrepreneurial business models and skills that sex workers in our interviews demonstrated reveal exactly how the Internet and digital technologies facilitate the making of money through a range of sexual services, sometimes in abstention. Our next chapter turns to mapping out these spaces, examining more closely how the Internet has structured online commercial sex spaces.

Note

1. We use the term cis-gendered to refer to people whose gender identity corresponds with the gender they were assigned at birth.

References

Association Chief Police Officers. 2010. *Setting the record straight. The trafficking of migrant women in England and Wales off-street prostitution sector.*

Bernstein, E. 2007. *Temporarily yours: Intimacy, authenticity and the commerce of sex.* Chicago: University of Chicago Press.

Brents, B., and K. Hausbeck. 2010. Sex work now: What the blurring of boundaries around the sex industry means for sex work, research, and activism. In *Sex work matters: Exploring money, power, and intimacy in the sex industry*, ed. M.H. Ditmore, A. Levy, and A. Willman. London: Zed Books.

Brents, B., and T. Sanders. 2010. 'The mainstreaming of the Sex industry: Economic inclusion and social ambivalence'. Special Issue for *Journal of Law & Society*; Regulating Sex/Work: From Crime Control to Neoliberalism 37 (1): 40–60.

Castells, M. 2000. *The rise of the network society: Information age: Economic, Society and culture.* London: Wiley, Blackwell.

Cunningham, S., and T.D. Kendall. 2011. Prostitution 2.0: The changing face of sex work. *Journal of Urban Economics* 69 (3): 273–287.

Hughes, D. 2004. The use of new communication technologies for sexual exploitation of women and children. In *Not for sale: Feminists resisting prostitution and pornography*, ed. R. Whisnant, and C. Stark. Toronto: Spinifex Press.

Import.io. 2014. Available at: https://matthew-painter.squarespace.com/post/gender-differences-amongst-sex-workers-online. Accessed 21 Mar 2017.

Lee-Gonyea, J.A., T. Castle, and N.E. Gonyea. 2009. Laid to order: Advertising on the Internet. *Deviant Behavior* 30: 321–348.

Lerum, K., and B.G. Brents. 2016. Sociological perspectives on sex work and human trafficking. *Sociological Perspectives* 59 (1): 17–26.

Mai, N. 2009. *Migrants in the UK Sex Industry: Final policy relevant report*, Institute for the Study of European Transformations, London Metropolitan University. http://archive.londonmet.ac.uk/iset/research-units/iset/projects/esrc-migrant-workers.html. Accessed 21 July 2017.

Min, S.J. 2010. From the digital divide to the democratic divide: Internet skills, political interest, and the second-level digital divide in political Internet use. *Journal of Information Technology & Politics* 7 (1): 22–35.

Office for National Statistics Guidance. 2015. *Harmonised concepts and questions for social data sources; primary principles: Demographic information, household composition and relationships*, v3.2.

Pettinger, L. 2011. Knows how to please a man': Studying customers to understand service work. *The Sociological Review* 59 (2): 223–241.

Pitcher, J. 2014. *Diversity in sexual labour: An occupational study of indoor sex work in Great Britain*. PhD Thesis, November, University of Loughborough. Available at: https://dspace.lboro.ac.uk/2134/16739.

Pitcher, J. 2015a. Direct sex work in Great Britain: Reflecting diversity. *Graduate Journal of Social Sciences* 11 (2): 76–100.

Pitcher, J. 2015b. Sex work and modes of self-employment in the informal economy: Diverse business practices and constraints to effective working. *Social Policy and Society* 14 (1): 113–123.

Platt, L., P. Grenfell, C. Bonell, S. Creighton, K. Wellings, J. Parry, and T. Rhodes. 2011. Risk of sexually transmitted infections and violence among indoor-working female sex workers in London: The effect of migration from Eastern Europe. *Sexually Transmitted Infections* 87 (5): 377–384.

Ray, A. 2007. Sex on the open market: Sex workers harness the power of the Internet. In *C'lick me: A netporn studies reader*, ed. K. Jacobs, M. Janssen, and M. Pasquinelli, 45–68. Amsterdam: Institute of Network Cultures.

Sanders, T. 2005a. It's just acting': Sex workers' strategies for capitalizing on sexuality. *Gender, Work and Organization* 12 (4): 319–342.

Sanders, T. 2005b. *Sex work: A risky business*. Cullompton: Willan Publishing.

Sanders, T. 2006. Sexing up the subject: Methodological nuances in researching the female sex industry. *Sexualities* 9 (4): 449–468.

Sanders, T. 2008. *Paying for pleasure: Men who buy sex*. Cullompton: Willan Publishing.

Sharp, K., and S. Earle. 2003. Cyberpunters and cyberwhores: Prostitution on the Internet. In *Dot cons. Crime, deviance and identity on the Internet*, ed. Y. Jewkes. Cullompton: Willan Publishing.

Shaver, N. 2005. Sex work research: Methodological and ethical challenges. *Journal of Interpersonal Violence* 20 (3): 296–319.

Smith, N., and S. Kingston. 2015. *Policy-relevant report: Statistics on sex work in the UK*. Birmingham and Lancaster: Universities of Birmingham and Lancaster.

Thakor, M., and D. Boyd. 2013. Networked trafficking: Reflections on technology and the anti-trafficking movement. *Dialect Anthropology* 37: 277–290.
van Dijk, J. 1991/2012. *The network society*, 3rd ed. London: Sage.
Walby, K. 2012. *Touching encounters: Sex, work, and male-for-male internet escorting*. Chicago: University of Chicago Press.

2

The Digital Sexual Commerce Landscape

Abstract The diversity of online working practices is reflected in the huge proliferation of online spaces used to facilitate commercial sex. These are broken down, in this chapter, into twelve distinct categories which enable the organisational features of online sex markets to be explored. Platforms and websites adopt varying business models, which in turn impact on how sex workers use and interact with these different spaces. The mapping of online sex work will be problematised based on the difficulties in accurately estimating both the numbers of online sex workers and the extent of the online sex industry. The role of online spaces to facilitate community support and, to some extent, political activism among sex workers is discussed.

Keywords Escort directories/advertising platforms · Webcam platforms Multi-service adult entertainment platforms · Dating and hook-up platforms · Customer review forums · Individual sex worker websites Classified websites · Social media platforms/apps · Sex worker forums Content delivery platforms

Introduction

The diversity of online working practices is reflected in the huge proliferation of online spaces used to facilitate commercial sex. These are broken down, in this chapter, into twelve distinct categories which enable the organisational features of online sex markets to be explored. Platforms and websites adopt varying business models, which in turn impacts on how sex workers use and interact with these different spaces. The mapping of online sex work will be problematised based on the difficulties in accurately estimating both the numbers of online sex workers and the extent of the online sex industry. The role of online spaces to facilitate community support and, to some extent, political activism among sex workers is discussed. We demonstrate and argue these points using qualitative interview data from 62 sex workers, and survey data from 641 sex workers, along with knowledge gained from observing platforms and interviews with operators of platforms.

Online Sex Work Environments

The diversity in the types of work offered by online sex workers is reflected in the variety of online spaces that are used to provide or facilitate commercial sex transactions. Before discussing in more detail how Internet-based sex workers in the UK use online technology to market and advertise their services, it is first important to set out the nature and scope of the different online sex work environments. During the BtG study, we identified twelve distinct sex work-related online environments - escort directories, webcam platforms, multi-service adult entertainment platforms, dating/hook-up platforms with commercial advertising, dating/hook-up platforms without commercial advertising, customer review forums, agency websites, individual sex worker websites, classified websites, content delivery platforms, social media platforms and sex worker forums. Each of these will be discussed in detail below.

Escort Directories/Advertising Platforms

Escort advertising platforms are third party websites that allow sex workers who offer in-person direct sex work to create profiles to advertise their services. There are escort advertising platforms that are international, carrying adverts from sex workers all over the world; there are others that operate at a national level and others that operate at a more local level. Escort advertising is, by and large, stratified by gender. Some platforms carry adverts from sex workers of all genders with the option for clients to search under specific gender categories whilst other sites focus on particular gender groups with cis-gendered[1] female only spaces, cis-gendered male only spaces and sites targeted specifically at transgender (trans) sex workers. The sites identified in our research that are marketed as spaces for trans sex workers to advertise were predominantly targeted at, and used by, trans women. We did not identify any specialist sites in our research that are used exclusively or especially by trans men.

There are also escort advertising platforms that focus on niche markets, for example, women who identify as BBW (Big Beautiful Women), and those that are used by sex workers of specific racial and ethnic groups. As Amy (43, independent sex worker) says *'there's niche sites for everything, you know. There's sites for black women, sites for large women, sites for small women, sites for older women, younger women, red-haired women, Chinese women ... all sorts of things'*.

Escort advertising platforms adopt a range of different business models. Some operate on a subscription basis where the sex worker pays the platform for hosting any kind of advertisement. The owner of Platform 17 explains:

> So the escorts pay to advertise on the website. If you like I'm basically a ... classified ads [site], I just happen to specialise in escort ads. It's the same model. I have a website that's known for escorts, escorts pay to advertise on that site.

Other platforms are free for sex workers to advertise but offer paid upgrades, the so-called freemium business model. In this business model, it is perfectly possible for sex workers to pay nothing for their advert on the site but there are several paid options, which improve their likelihood of attracting clients. The owner of Platform 44 explained how the upgrades work:

> All the directories though are initially free for people to advertise on and they can be free on there all the time, but there are chargeable options and, so for instance … the chargeable options are, I want to be featured, so there's a charge for that, so there's a monthly charge, depending on how high up you want to be featured on it, and that will make sure, it gives you benefits including front page, you are listed before other escorts in the area that they might be searching at.

None of the sites we identified in our research charged clients to access the site. The owner of Platform 17 explained how, for him, making the site easily accessible to clients was a key business strategy because '*if you start introducing registration or make the process too complicated you are going to lose that business*'. The ease of accessibility on escort advertising platforms opens up a whole new field of free sexual content online that has contributed to the development of 'virtual cruising' as a new leisure activity where viewers look much more frequently than they engage in negotiations or purchases.

Webcam Platforms

Webcam platforms are sites dedicated to the facilitation of webcam shows, and they provide an interface between the webcam models and the customers. As the webcam model performs their show, it is simultaneously streamed via the webcam platform to the customer's device where they can watch it (and pay for it). There is a huge proliferation of webcam sites globally with certain market leaders that dominate the field (Weisman 2015). Like escort advertising platforms, webcam sites also adopt a range of different business models.

Some of the market leading webcam platforms operate on a business model that revolves around 'tips'. In these sites, a model performs their show in a public 'room'[2] that any customer can log into and watch free of charge. The customer then tips the model throughout the show using tokens that they purchase from the webcam platform. It is common practice for models to have targets for generating tips that are linked to certain aspects of their shows, for example, they may have a target for taking off items of clothing or linked to the performance of certain sexual acts. The models we spoke to talked about the importance of creativity in webcamming, especially in shows that revolve around tips, where it is crucial to be inventive about what you can offer in exchange for tips. Jane (29, webcam worker) talked about having a tip target for taking her clothes off and went on to describe how she generates other tips, saying, *you can get them to tip for anything, like I'm doing a fitness kick right now, so I'll have them tip to make me do squats and stuff*. Cara (19, webcam worker also providing other services) had a similar approach and talked about setting 'topics', which refer to the different performative acts that she can use to generate tips:

> So it's free to chat but you can set a topic or sort of things that you want to sell for tokens. Yeah, so I'll set a topic, say, a thousand tokens to do topless or something ... And then you do a striptease or whatever, and then you start a new topic. So that one might be—I don't know. You sort of think up your prices on the day really, I guess, but obviously then you just keep thinking of new ones.

Within websites that operate with this business model, the performers tend to receive a fixed amount of cash per token tipped to them by customers. The platform, however, sells tokens to customers at different bundled rates with a cheaper unit price the more tokens that are purchased. This means it is impossible to ascertain exactly what percentage of the platform's earnings is passed on to the performers.

Other platforms adopt a different business model where customers pay a per-minute rate to watch a show. In this approach, there is a distinction between group and private shows. Group shows are performed to more than one person, and each person watching is paying a per-minute rate. Private shows are performed to just one person. It was most common in our interviews for models to talk about setting different rates for public and private shows, with private shows being priced higher.

Some models described the public room/show as being more of a marketing space than a performance space. Kisses (32, independent sex worker also providing BDSM and webcam services) explains:

> ...with group mode, you set your own price. So I think I've got mine at £1.10 or something like that, and that's where they come in and you're fully clothed. You could be wearing, like, your lingerie, but you're not meant to be naked or anything like that. And you just talk to them, if they're wanting a cam show, what kind of thing they're into. So they might be vanilla or ... they might be fetish or they might just wanna talk (laughs)... if you wanna do a private show for them, so you wanna get a bit ruder, you can get them into private, which I have my prices private per minute to be in private. So I think it's like £2.20 ... and I'll be in there and I'll then take my clothes off and I will do shows in private mode for the higher price. Whereas in group mode I tend to just chat with them about normal things. (Kisses, 32, independent sex worker also providing BDSM and webcam services)

Rebecca (48, provides phone and instant message services), on the other hand, prefers to use the public room as a performance space and tries to get as many people as possible in the public room because the earning potentials are higher:

> ...when you're camming you don't really want to do private shows, what you want is a public room. Like not a public room, but a sort of public room where they're paying, full of customers. Because if you're getting for example one pound fifty a minute for everyone that's in the room but if they take you private you're only getting three quid, if you've got ten people in the room you're laughing, you're now on fifteen quid a minute. Yeah, so you basically want to keep it as busy as you can.

Spartan (25, independent sex worker also providing BDSM, massage, webcam and other services), a male sex worker, took a similar approach to Rebecca:

> You log onto the software in general and you can disable group mode or private mode. So if you were extremely popular and you knew that you could keep seven people on at one pound forty-nine per minute simultaneously throughout the night, you would disable private because you'd never make the same money from one person.

Each model is responsible for setting their own per-minute rates on the webcam sites, and Spartan noted that *'the standard rule of private is twice the price'* of public, which was reflected in our interviews. Webcam sites that operate using this business model tend to take a fixed percentage of the model's earnings. The actual percentage taken varies from site to site with Platform 42 taking a 65% share of the income generated by a model whilst Platform 1 takes just 30% for webcamming services on its site. Platform 46 has a tiered payment structure where the more income a model generates the higher their percentage share, with a model at the lowest earnings level taking 30% of the income they generate and those at the highest level taking 60%.

Multi-Service Adult Entertainment Platforms

The third category of online sex work space identified in our research is what we have labelled as 'multi-service adult entertainment platforms'. These are websites that offer a range of different sex work services within the one site. The market leading website in the UK, Platform 1, is an example of a multi-service adult entertainment platform and was used in some way or other by the vast majority of both our interview and survey participants. The following discussion uses Platform 1 as an illustration of this particular type of online space.

Platform 1 offers a range of services including escort advertising and webcamming services. It also connects sex workers offering phone chat and instant message services with clients and allows sex workers to make and upload content (photos and videos) that clients then pay to download. Paris describes the diversity of services that she is able to offer on Platform 1:

> Platform 1 is a very big umbrella company because it's not just the camming. I can do phone chat. I can do, I can sell movie clips. I can sell proper twenty-minute clips, which are more like something people buy a DVD, like a porn DVD. I can do specifically IM, which is a type of just text-style chat. That's the one I predominately use the most. A lot of people, myself included, we rely heavily on that. So when Platform 1 goes down, we're all like, oh my god, we can't make no money, and we're all on Twitter having a rant. (Paris, 33, webcam worker also providing BDSM services)

Platform 1 earns income in a number of ways. First, it offers upgrades for additional services available to the escorts (providing direct services) who advertise on the site. For example, it is possible for a sex worker to pay a fee to have their advertisement placed at the top of the list of escorts in their particular area. Another common upgrade on Platform 1 is for the sex worker to pay a small daily fee to have their phone number visible on their profile. Without this upgrade, any communications between the client and sex worker would have to take place within the internal messaging system of the website.

Paying for upgrades on Platform 1 was very common amongst our sample. Ensuring that their profile was displayed prominently and accessible for clients was an important consideration for sex workers given the high number of profiles on the website. Cait described the advantages of paying for an upgrade to be listed on the first page of escorts in her local area:

> Because it saves people then trawling through page after page, especially if they are looking for somebody in general, rather than being specific, because obviously I don't fall into a lot of peoples' categories being the type of escort I am, but however, if somebody searches specifically for one thing then my details could come up, the same as, you know, hundreds of others. (Cait, 52, independent sex worker also providing webcam and other services)

Webcamming services on Platform 1 operate on a pay-per-minute basis with the sex worker setting their own rates. In addition to earning revenue through upgrade fees for escort advertising, Platform 1 also takes a percentage of all other monies earned by the sex worker through providing indirect services, such as webcamming, phone chat, instant message and content delivery. This percentage cut is currently around 30%.

The fact that a range of different services are available within the one website is, according to Platform 1, one of the keys to its success:

> There have always been directories, clipsites, cam sites, phone sex, back page advertising, sex toy stores, online marketplaces but Platform 1 was the first and remains the only website that brings all of these together in

one place. There have been many copycats over the years, some good but without the advertising or marketing savvy to get both sides of the customer base.

The suggestion, in the quote above, that Platform 1 is a market leader in multi-service adult entertainment platforms was absolutely reflected in both our qualitative and quantitative research. This will be outlined in more detail below in our mapping of the UK online sex industry.

Dating and Hook-up Platforms with Commercial Advertising

Dating and hook-up platforms have become an increasingly mainstream feature of social and cultural life (Gardner and Davis 2013). Whilst the primary purpose of dating and hook-up platforms is to facilitate the connection between people for personal relationships and unpaid sexual encounters, some of these platforms have designated commercial advertising space where sex workers can openly advertise their services. The number of dating/hook-up platforms openly allowing escort advertising is, however, relatively small compared to the overall number of these platforms in operation.

The only platforms identified in our research that allowed adult advertising were sites targeted at men who have sex with men. Platform 18 was discussed in our interviews (with male sex workers) as one of the few dating/hook-up sites that permits commercial advertising but Liam (38, provides massage services) suggested that its business model was failing:

> I don't think at the moment Platform 18's prices are fair because Platform 18's … business model has just disintegrated … it's a hook-up site and it's been taken over by location-based apps. When I first advertised on Platform 18, I would get a hundred views a day. At the moment, when I stopped advertising, my profile was lucky if I got one or two profile views a day … I honestly believe it's largely down to traffic.

None of the location-based dating/hook-up apps that Liam refers to in his quote permit open advertising for commercial sex, and this is likely because of the policies put in place to have an app approved for download in the Apple or Google Play app stores. For example, Apple's approval policy states that 'apps that solicit, promote, or encourage criminal or clearly reckless behavior will be rejected'.[3] This is obviously a very broad condition but taken together with Apple's prohibition on 'overtly sexual or pornographic material' makes a sex work advertising app virtually impossible. Google Play has an even more explicit policy, and it forbids any apps that 'promote escort services or other services that may be interpreted as providing sexual acts in exchange for compensation'.[4]

There are, however, new generations of sex work advertising apps being developed most notably German-based Peppr and Oh La La. Due to the restrictive policies on the app stores, these new apps are all web-based, which means that they are simply websites that have been optimised for use on a mobile device rather than a 'native app' that is designed for use on a device, i.e. all the apps available on Google Play and the Apple iTunes store.

Oh La La: Blurring the Line Between Sex Work and Dating

Pia Poppenreiter, a digital entrepreneur based in Germany, has launched two of the most innovative sex work advertising apps over the past couple of years. Peppr was launched in 2014 amidst a storm of publicity as it was labelled the 'Tinder for sex workers' (Prigg 2014) and was marketed as 'a mobile app that mimics the dating website model concept to connect prostitutes with prospective clients' (Brazil Bautista 2014). Poppenreiter claims that her inspiration for creating Peppr came from seeing sex workers working on the streets of Berlin:

> On a late autumn day in Berlin, I was on my way with a friend to a bar on Oranienburger Strasse. 'It was cold - I had a skirt on myself - and I saw a sex worker on the street. 'I thought, 'It's crazy that there's an app for everything, but not for that. 'Why do they have to stand there in the winter all day?' That thought never left me. (Prigg 2014)

Peppr makes money by charging a 10 EUR fee for each inquiry sent on the app. The clients send an inquiry to the sex worker advertising, and then, they communicate directly to set up the terms of their meeting. The escort keeps 100% of the fee paid for their services. The innovation of Peppr is its use of GPS location-based technology with the customer seeing the profiles of sex workers listed based on their physical distance from each other.

After reportedly running into operational difficulties with Peppr, Poppenreiter regrouped and launched Oh La La in August 2015, which was billed as a service that facilitated 'paid dating'. Oh La La is marketed very differently from Peppr with a clear intent to distance itself in its promotional material from any reference to escorting and sex work. As one commentator noted, 'the website is pink and white, not red and black. Everything is cuddly and not at all indecent' (Lohaus 2015).

Oh La La is currently available in a number of German cities, and a launch in New York City was attempted but at the time of writing appears no longer to be operating there.[5] The mechanics of Oh La La are quite different from Peppr. Men looking for 'paid dates' put out a request on the platform—they will specify the length of the date they are looking for, their requirements for the date and budget. This request remains live on the platform for 21 minutes during which time women can respond. Responding to the date then opens up a private chat between the two parties to discuss the terms in more detail. Women offering paid dates have much more control and privacy as their profiles are not public, and they do not receive any unsolicited messages or enquiries. Women advertising for dates are only visible to potential 'clients' once they have responded to a request (Ljunberg 2017).

Dating and Hook-up Platforms Without Commercial Advertising

Whilst Oh La La blurs the line between dating and sex work, it is still very clear that any 'dates' arranged on the site include a financial or commercial element. Other dating and hook-up sites, however, have very clear policies prohibiting any kind of advertising for paid sex on their sites. The presence of such a policy, however, does not mean that commercial sex is never advertised on these platforms. Instead, any commercial advertising that is undertaken is done covertly as Andy (57, independent sex worker also providing massage services) explains:

> These websites generally have in their terms and conditions that you can't offer any services for commercial gain. I mean, there's ways round it. You see some adverts it's just got, like, the profile name and pounds signs at the end, and I think it would be understood that that lad wants paying. But if they monitored that, they'd take that down.

Andy alludes to active enforcement by dating platforms of their bans on commercial advertising. A member of the staff of Platform 45, which is primarily a gay dating site, and explicitly forbids escort advertising, described how their policy is enforced:

> We're not really allowing that [escort advertising], so we have to make sure that it doesn't happen, even under the radar and the way we do that, we have, a system that kind of flags certain behaviour, and we have a very, very good user base who is reporting any kind of activity. So that's been kind of, always part of our site that, because you know, since we are operating in many countries with lots of users, we've always used our user base to actually monitor the site ... if there's any kind of activity on the site that's not according to the rules and regulations of our site, there's a function that they can report it to our customer service team and they, like they get rewarded with free membership if the report is valid.

Despite these policies and attempts at enforcement, it was clear from our research that commercial services were advertised on many dating and hook-up platforms, and that covert use of dating sites in this way appeared to be more common amongst male sex workers.

Customer Review Forums

A customer review forum is an online space where customers post messages about their experiences of buying sexual services (normally in-person) including reviews of individual sex workers that they have visited. Review forums, as well as being a space for customers to share experiences, are also a key marketing space for sex workers. Some forums have escort directories/escort advertising integrated into the platform. Sex workers, at least on some platforms, are also welcome to join the discussion side of the forum and can post messages and interact with clients, which acts as a subtle form of advertising.

Review forums were a significant subject of discussion in our qualitative interviews, primarily with female sex workers. Review forums used by clients of male sex workers are rare although a US-based forum for male sex work does, according to Rab (38, independent sex worker also providing massage services), have a *'growing base, particularly for London escorts'*. Our research highlighted that the UK-based forums used by male clients of cis-female sex workers have quite distinct and diverse online cultures. Eloise (37, independent sex worker providing massage services) explains the differences between forums:

> To use sort of industry terminology you get the fluffier sites shall we say where the balance seems to be more in favour of the working girl than it is the client. Then you get the ones that are in the middle where it's quite balanced… Then you get the other end of the extreme where the punter is king. All working girls are lying, thieving, see you next Tuesdays and the punters are perfect. And that seems to be crux of it. Then you get the ones that are quite mixed which is more about having a bit of laugh and a flirt sort of thing. They've all got different tones.

As Eloise's description alludes to there are certain forums where sex workers are welcomed, treated with respect by the customers and harassment and abuse are not tolerated or part of the online culture. On the other hand, there are examples of review forums in which stigmatising, misogynistic posts, effectively the online abuse and harassment of sex workers, is supported and encouraged by the culture of the forum. Platform 40 was raised by our interview participants countless times as an example of this type. Amber (25, independent sex worker also provides BDSM, massage and other services) describes Platform 40 as a *'misogynistic cess pool'*, Katy (30, agency-based sex worker) notes that this site '*doesn't like what they call fluffy reviews, which is where someone's nice*' and Kendall (29, independent sex worker) said that the customers that use this forum '*rip girls apart*'. Racist and anti-migrant posts were also a strong theme identified as frequent on some of these forums.

Whilst these forums exist, it is important to point out that many of the sex workers we interviewed described the clients who are active on forums, especially the more harmful ones, as a substantial minority of clients. Alice (46, independent sex worker providing other services) suggested that the clients who post on forums '*aren't normal clients … I don't know, they're fucking whore anoraks. They're weird*', and Katy (30, agency-based sex worker) described these clients as '*a subsection, they're all … quite culty, or cliquey*'. Also, some noted that amongst forum users were a section of more sympathetic and respectful customers. Our survey with customers showed that whilst browsing on forums was widely practiced only a minority of customers write reviews.

Agency Websites

Agency websites are run and controlled by third party agencies who act as intermediaries between sex workers who provide direct in-person services and their clients. The agencies are responsible for the running of the websites, which are used to advertise different sex workers working for the agency. This means that the sex workers have little involvement in the marketing of themselves online as this is all done by the agency. Whilst agency sex work was not a focus of our research we did interview a small number of sex workers who worked for an agency, one described how the agency takes responsibility for all the online marketing:

> So I'm getting some [photos] done at the beginning of December – we have to do that, but then they [the agency] pick them, do the editing, they write our profiles. That's a difficult one. Well it's okay, you know, they're very nice, my profile but their spelling isn't so great and, you know, you can't say to somebody, 'You've spelled that wrong,' because you're relying on them for jobs and no one wants to be told their spelling's no good. (Katy, 30, agency-based sex worker)

Although Katy's complaint over spelling may be minor, her description of the dynamics of agency work, and fear of antagonising the agency, highlights potential challenges for sex workers if they were unhappy with how they were being represented online. On the other hand, having minimal involvement in marketing and client screening is often one of the motivations for sex workers to opt for agency work rather than being independent. Katy talked about switching from independent work to agency work precisely because it was easier and *'you don't have to mess around with, dealing with timewasters and that kind of thing'*.

Individual Sex Worker Websites

This term refers to websites that are used to market individual sex workers who work independently. These websites are created and managed by the sex workers themselves or by web designers/IT specialists on their behalf. Individual websites are most often used by sex workers offering direct sexual services, namely, escorting, erotic massage and BDSM services. In our interviews, none of the people who *only* offered indirect services such as webcamming, phone chat and instant message had their own website. Around 29 per cent ($n = 185$) of those who responded to our survey stated that they had their own website, which suggests that this form of marketing is a substantial element of sex work advertising in the UK. Of the 185 sex workers who had their own website, four of them undertook only webcam work, confirming the propensity for individual websites to be used to market direct services.

Classified Websites

Classified websites are online advertising spaces/forums that allow individuals to post user generated advertisements for a range of goods and services. Some classified sites permit sex work advertising and have dedicated and separate space for these whilst others prohibit it altogether. It is usual business practice for classified sites to impose charges for certain types of ads (the remainder of posts being free), and adult advertising is one of these chargeable services. Allowing open adult advertising and charging commensurate fees has the potential to generate significant revenue for classifieds platforms. For example, one classified site advised us in an interview that a substantial portion of the site's revenue comes from adult advertising despite their website featuring a range of generic advertising. The fact that other classified sites forbid advertising for commercial sexual services means that sex workers, if they choose to use these sites, must post covertly, under other categories, such as 'health and beauty services' or under the 'personals' section, reflecting more subtle and covert traditional methods observed in the 1970s in newspaper columns, for instance.

Content Delivery Platforms

The ability to record and sell homemade videos to customers was mentioned by many of the sex workers we interviewed as a valuable source of extra income. Whilst some sex workers upload and sell photos and clips on escort advertising sites, there are also dedicated platforms that host and sell user-generated adult content online. We label these websites as 'content delivery platforms'. The sex worker creates their own content and the site simply hosts this and provides all the necessary technology and financial services for clients to purchase this content. The platform takes a percentage of any sale, and the sex worker is entirely in control of adding or deleting content from their profile on the site.

Jane (29, webcam worker) discussed the pricing systems on these platforms and noted that, whilst they impose a minimum pricing structure, beyond this, individuals are free to set their own prices. She, for example, sells her videos *'at two dollars higher than the minimum'*. The platform Jane described takes forty per cent of any earnings, which she felt was a fair split because *'the traffic that is on this website is fantastic. I have to do no promotion of my own ... and it just trickles in. The site is fantastic, it's worth it, definitely'*. Other sites have less traffic, and Cara (19, webcam worker) described how the site she used to sell content had less traffic, and as a result, she felt, *'you've got to sort of bring your own traffic over'*, which she did using social media.

Social Media Platforms/Apps

Our research shows that sex workers engage with social media in a range of diverse ways, and mainly because advertising spaces we have identified in this chapter have a strong social media presence. There were many sex workers in our sample who chose not to engage with social media at all in their working life. The reasons for making this decision almost always revolved around privacy concerns. Amongst the sex workers who did use social media in their work, there were varying degrees of engagement. Some used Twitter simply to communicate information to clients, for example, to keep clients up to date with their availability or to let them know whenever they log onto their webcam and are ready to start work. Others saw social media, especially Twitter use, as a way of building up, as Spartan (25, independent sex worker providing BDSM, webcam, massage and other services) describes *'an online brand'*. Some used Instagram and Snapchat for brand and sales. There was a strong perception amongst social media users that having a presence on social media contributed to building trust amongst clients.

Using Twitter to communicate with other sex workers, instead of, or as well as, clients was another common theme that arose in qualitative interviews. Some sex workers used their friendships with other sex workers on social media as a specific marketing strategy:

> I mainly use [Twitter] to engage with other models, cos people absolutely love the engagement between models. Especially when they think that we're all friends. Like my best friend, she's also a cam model, so we really monetise on our friendship. We'll send Tweets together and Snaps together and everyone wants us on cam together, and it never happens, but they just love the fact that we're friends. (Laughs) (Anne, 25, webcam worker)

For others, social media was a way to connect with fellow sex workers but not as a marketing strategy but more for peer support and friendship. Marcus (42, independent sex worker/escort and sexual massage provider), for example, said he finds Twitter *'particularly helpful in networking with other sex workers'*, and Amber (25, independent sex worker also provides BDSM, massage and other services) thought that Twitter, as an online networking space, is *'really, really good for sex workers'*.

Sex Worker Networking Online: Peer Support and Advocacy

Sex worker-led and peer support, initiatives, organisations and movements have been present in the UK for decades (Lopes 2006; AHRTAG/NSWP 1997). Our research illustrates how online technology has further enabled sex workers to organise, support each other share information about marketing, safety, rights and a wide range of work-related matters. A question Jones (2015) identified as unanswered by research about digital technology and sex work was how the shift to what she referred to as more isolated digitally mediated spaces had impacted on 'the ability of sex workers to forge and maintain social networks with one another' (Jones 2015, p. 559). Our research throws some light on this. Virtual networking with other sex workers and online peer support were key themes emergent from our interview and survey data which found sex workers have used a range of online platforms, social media and other applications to create online communities as vehicles for professional networking and peer support. One of the reasons the Internet was important to sex workers was its role in facilitating access to peer support: 80.7 per cent ($n = 517$) of survey respondents strongly agreed or tended to agree that the Internet gave them access to networks and peer support, and only 3.7 per cent ($n = 24$) disagreed or strongly disagreed.

When survey participants were asked about the main online platforms they used for advice or support, those identified by the highest proportion of respondents were sex worker forums, where information, advice and support is provided by other sex workers (Fig. 2.1).

Identified by 45.7 per cent ($n = 211$) of respondents, Platform 46 was the most utilised: a forum bearing the similar name of a market leading advertising platform for sex workers (Platform 1), but separate from it. Service providers who use Platform 1 can join and share information and advice on a range of sex work-related matters. Proportionately, more transgender and female respondents used this forum 52.9% ($n = 9$) and

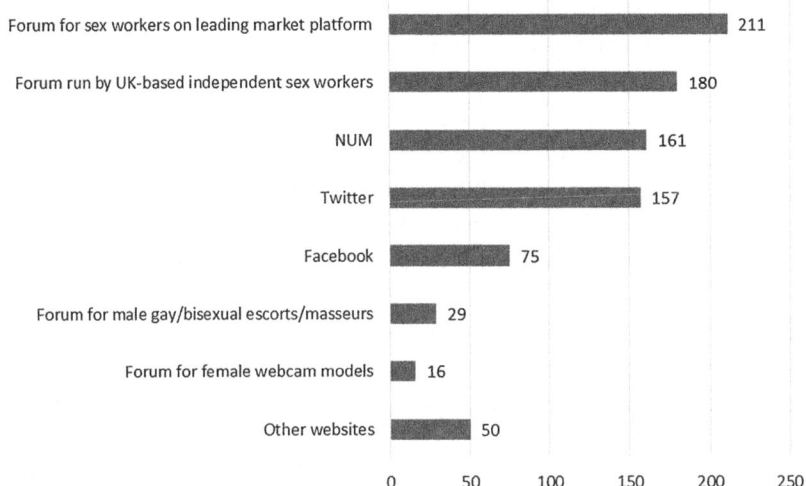

Fig. 2.1 Online spaces sex workers use for support and information

49% ($n = 177$), respectively (making it the most popular online source of advice or support for these two groups), compared to 27.9% ($n = 17$) for male participants, the third most popular source for men. Most of our male respondents used sites specifically for male-to-male sex work in their marketing, and thus were less likely to use Platform 1. Sex workers in interviews who used this forum valued the advice from other sex workers, and this forum was considered particularly useful for resolving technical or other difficulties with the advertising platform. There are several other forums utilised by sex workers for advice about how to make the best use of specific online advertising platforms.

A number of sex worker-led forums have been established by sex workers in the UK which aim to facilitate peer information sharing and support. Sex workers can register, read threads that relate to issues they are interested in, post a request for advice or send personal messages to specific members. The second online platform most identified for advice by 39 per cent ($n = 180$) of respondents was one of the longest established sex worker forums. Platform 47, a website (with a range of information for escorts) and a forum established over a decade ago by UK-based independent sex workers, has a range of boards including a 'Q&A' area where members can seek advice on any sex work-related topic, a popular

'Warnings and Wasters' section, a 'Find a Buddy' board and one for more light-hearted sex work-related discussions. This was the second most popular source of support identified by women in our survey with 45.7 per cent ($n = 165$) noting use, while only 6.6 per cent ($n = 4$) of men and 11.8 per cent ($n = 2$) of transgender respondents identified this. Whilst open to sex workers of all gender identities, this was not as popular for transgender and male respondents, being perceived as a forum historically for female sex workers, with other forum options targeted at male sex workers.

In 2010, Platform 48 was established as a forum specifically for UK-based gay and bisexual male escorts and masseurs who work with male clients. It aims to provide an online space where male escorts and masseurs can discuss a wide range of matters related to their sex work—6.3 per cent ($n = 29$) of participants were using this for advice and support. Amongst male respondent, over a third (39.3 per cent, $n = 24$) used it, and it was the most popular form of support for male sex workers in our survey. Forums play an important role in fulling the advice and support needs of a considerable section of sex workers.

The key reasons why sex workers used forums included for practical information and advice on a wide range of work-related matters (from advice on webcams, lighting, hotels to use for bookings to the law), a sense of connection and community, to reduce physical and social isolation (especially for those who were lone working and/or not out about their sex work) and to let off steam, sharing frustrations and light-hearted moments with colleagues and for some friendship. The safety benefits of engaging with forums were a key reason for participation (see Chap. 4). Forums were identified as particularly useful for 'newbies'—people new to sex work—or those considering working in the sector, for whom they could be a rich source of information and advice from people with experience of the sector. Male sex workers using Platform 48 valued its specific focus on male escorting and massage service providers, which meant their concerns were central. The forums people used were shaped by the sex work job they performed and gender identity; some forums have been developed specifically for certain sectors or were perceived to be for certain groups of sex workers. In survey open response data and interviews, respondents pointed to a range of forums utilised, which were specifically for erotic dancers, webcammers (e.g. Platform 49 used by a small section, 3.5 per cent ($n = 16$) of female webcammers), BDSM providers and other specialist jobs which provided information and support from others in the same sex work job.

Amongst our interview participants, the extent to which sex workers utilised sex worker forums was variable, with three main categories: non participants, occasional participants who dipped into such forums and frequent participants who logged on more regularly and tended to be more active participants. Reasons for non use varied: Some people felt they had adequate knowledge borne out of their own experience of sex work, some were concerned engagement could compromise privacy and anonymity, others were deterred by what they perceived as etiquette, tensions and conflicts that could be encountered within forums. Some participants were aware of forums but had not used them but would if they needed support, and others preferred to access information and support via other means including smaller online groups and personal networks of sex workers.

Sex workers in our research used social media not only for marketing and communication with clients but also for professional networking and support. In our survey, 34 per cent ($n = 157$) said they used Twitter and 16.2 per cent ($n = 75$) used Facebook for advice and support. Twitter was the fourth most popular source overall for support and Facebook the fifth overall. Whilst numbers of respondents were small, amongst intersex and non-binary respondents 76.9 per cent ($n = 10$) identified Facebook and 61.5 per cent ($n = 8$) identified Twitter, making these social media platforms the first and second ranked sources of support for this cohort. For transgender respondents, Twitter was ranked second and Facebook was ranked third as a source of support. Social media and free messaging apps such as WhatsApp have been embraced by a section of sex workers to create several private peer support and networking groups. These groups and the diversity of networks have received less attention in research. In our study, some of these had a large membership and geographical reach, and others were smaller and localised or were formed by small groups of close colleagues or friends working in the sector.

> I'm in touch with two girls. One I met via Twitter. I'm in touch with her daily. And another girl who used to work in a flat I used to work in ... we're in contact through Twitter now,. I give her a lot of help ...

> There is peer support going on. (Slapper, 60, independent, webcammer, dominatrix)
>
> I'm very active on a Facebook group … I'm one of the admin people… Platform 56 … There's 520 members. (Michael, 57, independent)
>
> I have a strong WhatsApp groups of other sex workers who are my main support. (Female survey respondent, 25–34, Webcamming, phone sex work, adult film industry/porn, modelling (glamour/erotic), BDSM)

Whatever the size of these networks and their scope for members, they are important sources of information, peer support, solidarity and community that reduce isolation and provide safety benefits. Indeed, many of the benefits identified for sex worker forum use were the same reasons given for use of networks formed around social media platforms:

> I am actually part of a private Facebook group which kind of developed from Twitter. We're like a secret group … there's about a hundred and thirty people … although people do put warnings in, it's more of like a support group … like a solidarity thing. So I don't tend to use the boards so much now. (Amber, 25, independent sex worker also provides massage, BDSM and other services)

Social media facilitated networks provide free information, advice and support from peers, which is easily and rapidly accessible. For some, these spaces provided a more personalised support than a larger forum:

> There's about three-hundred of us, … the sex work support Facebook group is pretty much the main crux of it…, a lot of people report feeling isolated but I don't really, because I have this kind of immediate access to hundreds of people that are in the same situation… I have a question just shoot it off and get a response in a bit … you also get a lot of support that feels a lot more personal because you tend to know them rather than kind of anonymous user names on a forum. (Bethany, 20, Independent)

Our research has taken place at a time when significant numbers of sex workers are using social media for peer support, and our findings illustrate how, for many sex workers, the use of social media for online sex worker networking is now an important aspect of communication and virtual community building for sex workers. An independent escort described social media platforms as *'online water coolers'* for sex workers; this description is apt for these and other sex worker online spaces, which offer a place where a group of workers can come together share concerns about work and socialise.

Activism Online

Jones (2015) posited that despite the political benefits for sex workers of the Internet, social research has not explored the role online technology has played in sex work activism. Ray (2007) identified activism as part of the online shift for sex workers, with the speed and reach of the Internet allowing *'collaborations … to happen in a powerful way, sex worker activism online has not just been about chatting and emailing, but about real coalition building'* (p. 66). Our research suggests that for sex workers in the UK, online spaces have provided a platform for campaigns for sex worker rights and for challenging UK government policies, media/cultural misrepresentations and stereotypes of sex workers.

Only a minority of participants in our research identified themselves as being involved in sex worker rights groups as activists but there was a larger group who took an interest in sex worker rights issues and sex work policy developments. They accessed news, followed social media accounts, websites or blogs of particular sex worker rights advocacy groups or individual sex workers. Heather used Twitter *'to keep up to date with activism… I have a Facebook account now … to read and see what other sex workers are posting about'* (Heather, 31, independent escort). This ability of sex workers to engage with sex worker rights issues and debates via online technology meant that they can stay informed about rights-based issues and feel connected to a wider activist community. Digital technology has the advantage of enabling sex workers who are spread throughout the UK to follow activism and sex worker rights issues, and for those who are not out about their sex work, or who wish not to be identified, to be politically informed with relative anonymity.

Minichiello et al. (2015, p. 8) observed that *'the Internet has strengthened efforts to coordinate the political activity of sex workers nationally and internationally'*. Those in our research who identified as involved in sex worker activism flagged the importance of online communication for activism. Online technology is central for the day-to-day functioning and organising of sex worker rights organisations in the UK, much activism is online and organising can be carried out via both public and private groups on social media and a range of platforms can be used to communicate their messages. All key sex worker rights organisations[6] in the UK, during our research, had a relatively strong online and social media presence, with websites, Twitter and Facebook accounts, and some utilising Instagram, Tumblr and other applications. Social media platforms have created myriad possibilities for organising amongst sex worker groups and organisations. They enable organisations to communicate with members and allies (getting information, e-newsletters, blogs out to followers and the general public quickly), to host and share resources, fundraise and promote campaigns, activities and events.

During Beyond the Gaze, there were several high-profile UK-based campaigners who utilised online platforms, social media and blogging to raise awareness about sex worker rights issues and the campaigns they were involved with. Laura Lee[7], who was challenging through the high courts in Northern Ireland the law that made it a crime to pay for sexual services, used online crowdfunding to support her challenge and social media was utilised to raise awareness about her concerns with the law and its impact on the safety and rights of sex workers. Charlotte-Rose a sex worker and campaigner, with 19700 Twitter followers and her own radio show, has utilised social media and online radio to promote sex worker rights, for example, promoting campaigns opposing the Audio Visual Media Services Regulations which banned the depiction of a range of acts, for example, the face sitting[8] protest outside the House of Commons. Blogging (Feldman 2014) and in our research vlogging (video blogging) were used to create a voice for sex workers and a space for activism, challenging whorephobic and stereotypical images and discourses. Blogs provide a space for sex workers' perspectives and when her fetish, queer porn website 'Dreams of Spanking' was taken down and investigated by the Authority for Television on Demand, Pandora Blake blogged and vlogged about the case and continues to campaign as a spokesperson for Backlash.[9] There are several platforms sex workers have used for online video content in advocacy, for example, in 2016 Juno Mac a sex worker activist filmed a TED talk '*The laws that sex workers really want*'[10] and at the time of writing, this had over 1,760,000 views, demonstrating the extensive reach online activism can have.

Providing a space where sex workers can take control of their own cultural representation is another way online technology has been used by sex workers in the UK. A range of sex worker-led cultural and arts initiatives, which provide a vehicle for sex workers' voices and challenge stigma and stereotypes, now utilise online and digital technology as an integral element of their marketing and awareness raising. For example, the Sex Workers Opera (SWO),[11] '*a multidisciplinary show created and performed by sex workers and friends*', utilised social media and online technology as an integral part of its development, marketing and advocacy work, and productions have been supported partially by online crowdfunding.

Online spaces are being utilised creatively by sex workers as a vehicle for advocacy and activism around sex worker rights, a tool for individual and collective voices.

Mapping the UK Online Sex Industry

Given the proliferation and transient nature of online advertising for sex work, it is impossible to provide a reliable quantitative mapping of online sex work in the UK, or indeed anywhere. Mapping populations of sex workers is notoriously difficult and challenging (Cusick et al. 2009), and this is no different in online environments. There are also valid questions to be asked about the use and value of population size estimates of sex workers and what purpose these serve (Global Network of Sex Work Projects 2015; WHO et al. 2013). The police, for example, have very different motivations for mapping the online sex industry from, say, health projects or sex worker support services. Police motivation for mapping the online industry may be a conduit to conducting enforcement action against online sex workers. One strategic police lead suggested:

> …basically I think essentially what a number of the forces are doing at the minute is they're just trying to map what is sex work like in their areas because we don't know, you know. And the tactics we use – that we've used to tackle sex working historically, you know, have driven it underground.

One method that could be used to map the online sex industry is simply to count the number of sex worker profiles/adverts on certain sites. This, however, will never provide a complete and accurate picture of the true extent of online sex work because:

- The number of sex worker profiles/adverts online does not necessarily translate into the number of sex workers actively working.
- Many of the adverts/profiles may be out of date and no longer active yet still appearing online.
- Some sex workers may have multiple profiles (e.g. for advertising different types of services) on the same platform and are highly likely to have profiles/adverts on multiple different sites.

From our sex worker survey responses, we were able to ascertain that the average (mean) number of sites used for advertising by each individual sex worker was three with only 32.8 per cent ($n = 210$) of respondents using just one advertising source. The potential for double or triple counting is therefore significantly high.

Another difficulty in assessing the extent of the online sex industry in the UK is the diversity and proliferation, as well as the internationalisation, of all adult platforms. This makes it impossible for us to provide an accurate estimation of the number of discrete websites and platforms used for commercial sex online. As well as websites that have national and international reach, there are also highly diversified local sites covering towns or regions in the UK. Furthermore, some platforms are widely known and used whilst others are more peripheral with limited reach and use. Whilst we did conduct our own searches to identify key sex work-related websites, and the data from our participants provided insight on the most widely used sites, we make no attempt to estimate the precise number of sex work-related platforms that are used by people operating in the UK. If we did make an estimate, we would be offering data that would be immediately out of date given the fluid and fragile nature of the sex markets online. We are very aware that in describing the online sex markets that any slight change in the law in any relevant jurisdiction could have significant effects on how advertising is organised online and the very presence of online sex work.

One major finding, however, that is obvious from both our qualitative and quantitative data is the importance of a handful of key market leading websites in the field of online commercial sex in the UK, especially for sex workers providing direct services. There is one particular market leading website that was identified as an advertising source by 93 per cent ($n = 436$) of the female sex workers who responded to our survey. Charlotte (35, independent sex worker providing BDSM and other services) described Platform 1 as having '*the monopoly*', and Kendall (29, independent sex worker) felt it was '*the Facebook of an escort directory*'. It was very common in interviews to hear some version of these comments from female sex workers:

> The biggest directory in England though is Platform 1, which is – without a double Platform 1 is the busiest. (Amber, 25, independent sex worker also provides massage, BDSM and other services)
>
> Essentially, I don't think I would get any bookings if I didn't advertise on [Platform 1] … I can't not advertise there, I feel everyone comes from there really. (Bethany, 20, independent)

Whilst Platform 1 is an advertising platform for all genders, our research shows that male sex workers, marketing themselves to other men, are more likely to use male specific escort directories than Platform 1. There was a clear market leading male escort advertising site identified in our research with 77 per cent ($n = 95$) of the male sex workers who responded to our survey indicating that they used this site. The use of Platform 1 amongst male sex workers was much less (33 per cent;

$n = 41$) but still represented a popular website for men according to the BtG survey results.

The numbers of trans-identified respondents to our survey were so low that we are unable to draw any conclusions from the survey results on advertising sources for transgender sex workers. In our qualitative interviews, however, the transgender women we interviewed identified Platform 1 again as their main advertising source. Specialist websites for transgender women were also used but there were mixed views on how successful these were. Victoria (19, independent sex worker) said that she used Platform 25, a specialist site for transgender women and that *'lots of people go there looking for transgender people'* whilst Dawn (49, independent sex worker) felt that the same website was *'very poor, both in response ratio and also quality of people'* and that when she gets enquiries from this site *'nine out of ten are absolute timewasters'*. We did not identify any site in our research that was marketed at transgender men and did not have any transgender men participants, in the interviews, so are unable to comment on the marketing practices of this group of sex workers.

Conclusion

The Internet has had an extraordinary and transformative impact on the sex industry globally, which is reflected in changes seen in the UK context. The Internet has transformed not only what services sex workers offer to their clients and how they offer them but has also created new opportunities for sex workers to connect and interact with each other in safe and anonymous ways. This has all been made possible because of the highly diversified range of online spaces that facilitate, or are connected to, commercial sex services. Despite this diversification and proliferation of online spaces, our research has shown that most commercial sex transactions in the UK are concentrated in a handful of market leading platforms. Reliance on the Internet for work is now widespread not only amongst those who provide their services in an online environment but also for independent indoor escorts who are often dependent on the Internet as a primary source of marketing and advertising.

Notes

1. We use the term cis-gendered to refer to people whose gender identity corresponds with the gender they were assigned at birth.
2. The webpage within the webcam platform that hosts the model's live stream is called their 'room'. When clients join the room, they can see the show and can communicate with the model through typing messages, which appears on a comment thread.
3. https://developer.apple.com/app-store/review/guidelines/#legal. Accessed 29th August 2017.
4. https://play.google.com/about/restricted-content/. Accessed 29th August 2017.
5. There is no information in the public domain about the reasons why the launch in NYC was unsuccessful. The legal context in NYC is obviously very different from Germany with commercial sex, in any form, a criminal offence.
6. SCOT-PEP, Sex Workers Alliance Ireland (which covers Northern Ireland as well as the Republic of Ireland) Sex Workers Advocacy and Rights Movement, English Collective of Prostitutes and x:talk.
7. https://www.theguardian.com/society/2017/apr/02/northern-ireland-sex-worker-overturn-ban-hiring-escorts. Accessed 1st June 2017.
8. http://www.independent.co.uk/voices/comment/ive-organised-a-mass-face-sitting-protest-outside-parliament-because-im-not-willing-to-give-up-my-9918757.html. Accessed 1st June 2017.
9. http://pandorablake.com/blog. Accessed 1st June 2017.
10. https://www.ted.com/talks/juno_mac_the_laws_that_sex_workers_really_want. Accessed 1st June 2017.
11. http://www.sexworkersopera.com/. Accessed 1st June.

References

AHRTAG/NSWP. 1997. *Making sex work safe*. London: Russell Press.
Brazil Bautista, C. 2014. Prostitution now has its own dating-style app—Yes, this is real. Available at http://www.digitaltrends.com/mobile/peppr-app-hooks-up-prostitutes-with-clients/. Accessed 12 May 2017.

Cusick, L., H. Kinnell, B. Brooks-Gordon, and R. Campbell. 2009. Wild guesses and conflated meanings? Estimating the size of the sex worker population in Britain. *Critical Social Policy* 29 (6): 703–719.

Feldman, V. 2014. Sex work politics and the internet. In *Negotiating sex work: Unintended consequences of policy and activism*, ed. C.R. Snowden and S. Majic, 243–266: Minneapolis: University of Minneapolis Press.

Gardner, H., and K. Davis. 2013. *The app generation: How today's youth navigate identity, intimacy, and imagination in a digital world*. New Haven: Yale University Press.

Global Network of Sex Work Projects. 2015. Mapping and population size estimates of sex workers: Proceed with extreme caution. Available at http://www.nswp.org/resource/mapping-and-population-size-estimates-sex-workers-proceed-extreme-caution.

Jones, A. 2015. Sex work in a digital age. *Sociology Compass* 9 (7): 558–570.

Ljungberg, E. 2017. Liquid, invisible and always available? Sex work and mobile communication. Paper presented at the Displacing sex Work conference, Aalborg University, Copenhagen March 15th 2017.

Lohaus, S. 2015. We talked to two escorts who actually use the 'Uber for Escorts'. http://motherboard.vice.com/read/we-talked-to-two-sex-workers-who-actually-use-the-uber-for-escorts. Accessed 12 May 2017.

Lopes, A. 2006. Sex workers and the labour movement in the UK. In *Sex work now*, ed. R. Campbell and M. O'Neill. Cullompton: Willan.

Minichiello, V., J. Scott, and D. Callander. 2015. A new public health context to understand male sex work. *BMC Public Health* 15 (282): 1–11.

Prigg, M. 2014. Forget cards in phoneboxes, now there's an app for that: Peppr service dubbed 'Tinder for sex workers' launches in Berlin (where prostitution is legal). http://www.dailymail.co.uk/sciencetech/article-2613634/Forget-cards-phoneboxes-theres-app-Peppr-app-dubbed-Tinder-sex-workers-launches-Berlin-prostitution-legal.html. Accessed 12 May 2017.

Ray, A. 2007. In *C'lickme: a netporn studies reader*, ed. K. Jacobs, M. Janssen, and M. Pasquinelli, 45–68. Amsterdam: Institute of Network Cultures.

Weisman, C. 2015. Inside the rapidly growing cam industry that's changing the porn industry as we know it Alternet http://www.alternet.org/inside-rapidly-growing-cam-industry-thats-changing-porn-industry-we-know-it. Accessed 11th May 2017.

World Health Organisation, United Nations Population Fund, Joint United Nations Programme on HIV/AIDS, Global Network of Sex Work Projects, World Bank and United Nations Development Programme. 2013. *Implementing comprehensive HIV/STI programmes with sex workers: Practical approaches from collaborative interventions.* Available at http://www.who.int/hiv/pub/sti/sex_worker_implementation/en/.

3

Characteristics and Working Practices of Online Sex Workers

Abstract This chapter reviews some of the core findings from the Beyond the Gaze dataset to consider the characteristics and working patterns of sex workers who market or provide services via the Internet. Specifically, this project has included sex workers of all genders, highlighting diverse practices and experiences when compared with the existing literature related to female sex workers. We examine the working practices (such as hours, pay, services and employment profiles) and broader socio-demographics of the sex work community, commenting on issues such as migrant sex workers' experiences and age differences. We also consider how the Internet has changed working practices in different sectors.

Keywords Diversity in sex work · Demographic characteristics
Gender · Working practices · Travel to work · Role of internet
Earnings · Independent sex work · Webcamming · Migrant workers

Introduction

This chapter reviews some of the core findings from the Beyond the Gaze (hereafter BtG) dataset to consider the characteristics and working patterns of sex workers who market or provide services via the Internet. Specifically, this project has included sex workers of all genders, highlighting diverse practices and experiences when comparing with the existing literature on female sex workers alone. We examine the working practices (such as hours, pay, services and employment profiles) and broader socio-demographics of the sex work community, commenting on issues such as migrant sex workers' experiences and age differences. We also consider how the Internet has changed working practices in different sectors.

Diversity of Sex Workers Using the Internet

Whilst there is limited robust baseline information currently (cf. Sharp and Earle 2003; Cunningham and Kendall 2011; Sanders et al. 2016), the data collected as part of the Beyond the Gaze study may be compared with earlier research into different groups of sex workers using the Internet for their work, which document their characteristics, working sectors and experiences (e.g. Koken et al. 2004; Cunningham and Kendall 2011; Jones 2015a). The survey of sex workers for this study provided a diverse sample in terms of gender, sexuality, age, ethnicity/ nationality and qualification levels. The profile of respondents, as shown in the Appendix, differed in many ways from the characteristics presented in policy reports, which are often based on studies of sex work in the street and managed indoor sectors, and demonstrated the importance of including Internet-based sex workers in analyses of the sex worker population. Moreover, as Jones (2015a) notes, even studies of sex workers using the Internet may not reflect the full diversity within digital sex work, in relation to factors such as ethnicity, gender, age and skills.

The gender composition of survey respondents in the BtG study reflected the feminised sexual labour workforce generally, with nearly three-quarters being female. Nonetheless, it is important to note that 19% were male, 3% transgender[1] and a further 3% non-binary or intersex. A small number of 'others' included those who defined themselves as gender fluid and respondents who only worked as part of a couple. The gender distribution appears to reflect findings from other studies estimating numbers of sex workers in the UK (e.g. Pitcher 2015a), which indicate that the proportion of women in the population of sex workers may be overestimated, particularly in relation to independent indoor-based sex work. Whilst policies are often directed at female sex workers, as Whowell and Gaffney (2009) have also argued, it is important not to neglect the service needs of sex workers of other genders.

Whilst 51.3% ($n = 239$) of female survey respondents gave their sexuality as straight/heterosexual and 43.6% ($n = 203$) as bisexual, only a very small number (less than 1%) identified as lesbian. This is comparable to other studies of female indoor-based sex workers which show diverse sexuality amongst their participants (e.g. Perkins and Lovejoy 2007; Koken 2012). Whilst the proportion of female participants identifying as lesbian was similar to that in the UK Annual Population Survey 2015 (ONS 2016), the proportion stating that they were bisexual was much higher than that in the national population estimates. In comparison, 63.7% ($n = 79$) of male BtG survey respondents identified as gay, 28.2% ($n = 35$) as bisexual and only eight respondents as heterosexual. Whilst the Annual Population Survey 2015 notes that males were more likely than females to identify as gay or bisexual, the number of men in these categories comprised a very small percentage of the population overall. Even taking into account the likelihood of under-reporting in the ONS survey, therefore, the profile of sex workers in the BtG study, particularly male participants, differs substantially from national studies exploring the sexual identity of the population as a whole. Other research studies of male sex work (e.g. Bimbi 2007; Whowell and Gaffney 2009) have noted that the majority of male sex workers identify as gay, and the profile of BtG survey respondents reflects this. This contrasts with studies drawing on single Internet advertising directories aimed primarily at the heterosexual market which, not surprisingly, have found a higher proportion of male sex workers identifying as straight/heterosexual (e.g. Smith and Kingston 2015).

The sexuality of respondents thus relates to the advertising sites discussed in Chap. 2, which reinforces the importance of using various sites to access sex workers, in order to capture the diverse population in Internet-based sectors.

Whilst survey respondents were not asked about client gender, 61 sex workers participating in interviews provided services to male clients. Additionally, ten provided services to female clients (this included two bisexual female sex workers) and 23 of all genders provided services to couples. There is a comparatively small body of literature on the provision of sexual services to women, although certain other studies have documented spaces of lesbian sex work. For example, Perkins and Lovejoy (2007) identified a proportion of female private sex workers in Australia providing services to other women, sometimes as part of a couple. Pilcher (2012) and Cole et al. (2015) also discuss the practice of employing female erotic dancers in some lesbian clubs.

Similar to other research studies of indoor sex workers (e.g. Sanders 2006; Jeal and Salisbury 2007), a large proportion of survey respondents entered sex work in their 20s or 30s. Only 5% ($n = 33$) started sex working when they were aged under 18; and 9.2% ($n = 59$) were aged 40 and above when they entered the industry. A considerable number of studies already exist which contradict assertions that most people who sell sex were children when they first entered the sex industry (see Comte 2014). Whilst sex workers across indoor sectors are seen to differ in their characteristics from street-based sex workers, there are also differences between those working in managed establishments and those working independently, including those who use the Internet for their work (Bernstein 2007a; Pitcher 2015b). For example, the age profile of Internet-based sex workers in studies of this group appears to show a slightly higher average age than for sex workers in other indoor settings (Koken 2012; Walby 2012). Whilst numbers are small, male survey respondents were more likely to enter sex work when younger than their female counterparts (nearly 15%; $n = 17$ were aged below 18, compared with only 3.4%; $n = 15$ of female sex workers). This corresponds with some other studies of male sex workers, which have suggested that the exchange of sex for incentives may sometimes form a part of early sexual experimentation (Bimbi 2007; Gaffney 2007).

3 Characteristics and Working Practices of Online Sex Workers

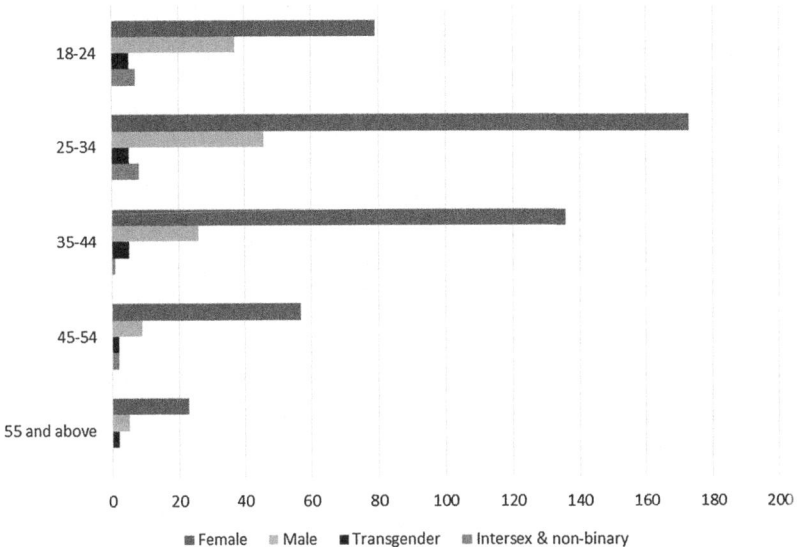

Fig. 3.1 Respondents' age group by gender. $N = 641$

There was considerable diversity in current age amongst survey respondents, with more than 60% ($n = 406$) of respondents aged between 25 and 44 at the time of the survey. Whilst male and female respondents were spread across different age groups, with the highest proportion of both gender groups in the age group 25–34, men were more likely than women to be concentrated in the younger age groups (Fig. 3.1). Whilst the respondent numbers are very small and, thus, it was necessary to combine some gender categories, it may be noted that the majority of transgender respondents (both male–female and female–male) were also distributed fairly evenly across the age groups 18–44.

There is far less information on the ethnicity of Internet-based sex workers. Certain studies (e.g. Murphy and Venkatesh 2006; Koken 2012) suggest that there is less ethnic diversity amongst Internet-based sex workers than in some other sectors, although Lee-Gonyea et al. (2009) found a range of ethnicities advertised amongst escorts on agency websites. A study by Jones (2015b) of the profile of female webcam models and erotic performers suggests that race has a bearing on webcam model success, with cam scores (website-generated measures of individual monetary success) being lower for black than for white women. As shown in the Appendix, the majority of survey respondents in the BtG study were white, although this included sex workers of British and non-British nationality. Nearly 15% ($n = 94$) of survey respondents overall were of non-UK nationality, with the proportion of those working exclusively as independent sex workers/escorts being 17.2% ($n = 31$), and for webcam/phone workers being 22.5% ($n = 16$). The majority of non-British survey respondents were from Eastern Europe, with a substantial number also from Western Europe and North America. A small number were from Asia, Australasia, Africa and the Indian subcontinent, and some were from Ireland. The proportion of non-UK respondents appears lower than the proportion of migrant sex workers in the UK estimated in other studies (e.g. Agustín 2006; TAMPEP 2007). It should be noted, however, that the survey sample was drawn from sex workers based across the UK and, as Pitcher (2015a) has observed, higher proportions of migrant sex workers are found in London than in many other parts of the UK. Furthermore, there have been no comparative quantitative research studies investigating the nationality of sex workers in different sectors in the UK, and it is possible that migrant workers may be less represented in independent indoor sectors. Jenkins (2009) points to factors such as lack of local knowledge for overseas students or migrant workers, which may prohibit establishing a sole self-employed venture. From the qualitative interviews for the BtG study, there was also an indication that some migrant workers might find it difficult accessing information and support, and that negotiating services with clients via the Internet could be problematic because of language barriers. For example, Milena commented that migrant sex workers would be less likely to participate in forums with clients:

> People that have difficulties with English language would not join, and even me at the beginning, that is also one of the reasons why I was – I did join because obviously I have the knowledge of how to do so. I would join but I wouldn't participate in a conversation as much because obviously I would be worried about is it relevant? Have I understood the topic

3 Characteristics and Working Practices of Online Sex Workers 61

correctly? Is my spelling okay? Am I going to represent myself as a person who is a total ditz and doesn't know what she's doing, right, because if you put yourself out there and you don't know the language it's quite difficult to kind of manipulate a conversation in the way that you could like interest the client a bit more. (Milena, 32, independent sex worker/escort also providing BDSM services)

Interview participants noted that suspicion of outsiders, not only the police but also others offering advice or support, could deter migrant workers from engaging with support services. This reluctance, compounded by language barriers and concerns over immigration status, is also reflected in other studies of migrant sex workers to the UK sex industry (e.g. Mai 2009). It should also be noted that the BtG online survey was not available in languages other than English, and thus non-English speakers will not have been able to participate. These factors also need to be taken into account in relation to responses to the survey, and thus it is difficult to draw conclusions on the ethnic composition of the Internet-based indoor industry from the profile of respondents.

It is interesting to note (see data in the Appendix) that survey respondents were comparatively highly qualified (37%; $n = 239$ were educated to degree level or higher; a further third ($n = 212$) possessing qualifications to A level or diploma level). There was no significant difference between males and females.[2] The level of educational capital amongst respondents corresponds with other studies of sex workers in indoor sectors, particularly independent sex work. For example, Bernstein (2007a), Bimbi (2007), Walby (2012) and Jones (2015a) all comment on the way in which Internet sex work attracts workers from diverse social classes. Over three-quarters of Walby's (2012) study of male sex workers had attained or were studying for a degree. In Jenkins' (2009) survey of 497 escorts advertising online, 35% of male participants were educated to degree level, with the proportion being slightly less for female participants (33%). These studies also test assumptions regarding the predominance of 'survival' sex work and, along with this current study, demonstrate the changing nature of sex work and the profile of sex workers, particularly Internet-based workers.

It is also worth noting that the majority of respondents did not have any financial dependents (two-thirds of females, $n = 310$; and 89% of males, $n = 109$). Although financial dependents may incorporate not only children but also adult dependents, this figure may be contrasted with studies of female sex workers in street or managed indoor sectors (e.g. Sanders 2005; Jeal and Salisbury 2007), which show a comparatively higher proportion of participants with young children, and potentially demonstrates a difference between sex workers in these sectors and those working independently online. Nearly 79% ($n = 142$) of survey respondents with financial dependents were aged 25–44, although as shown earlier, sex workers using digital technologies span all age groups. A few interview participants referred to the relative flexibility independent part-time sex work gave them to look after their children. For example, for Hannah, part-time webcam work suited her childcare responsibilities:

> I've just found out how easy it is and it's just, the technology is there in your phone, in your tablet, and it's all taken care of by a third party. So I can, you know, I can work whenever I feel like it and wherever I am. And, you know, when, when you're a bit skint, thirty quid can feed your family for a few days, so I can log on for half an hour and I can make that money and, within a week, it will be in my account. (Hannah, 34, webcam worker also providing BDSM services)

Emma (37, independent sex worker/escort) also commented that '*There's the freedom of sort of not being tied down with a company, you can pick and choose and work whenever you want to and to work it around my childcare as well*'. Nonetheless, she had some help with childcare from other family members and, as Pitcher (2015b) has noted, independent sex work may not always be compatible with raising young children, because of the unsocial hours involved. The profile of respondents indicates a need to consider the contemporary sex industry, particularly independent direct sex work and new types of Internet-facilitated work such as webcamming, and how this reflects changes to what was previously known about the sex industry, including the gender composition and relative circumstances of sex workers. These changes to the sex

3 Characteristics and Working Practices of Online Sex Workers 63

industry need to be set in the context of the developments in consumption and emergence of new social structures as a result of digital communication discussed in the Introduction to this book.

Place of Residence and Travel to Work

Survey respondents were based across the UK, with the highest proportions being in London, the South East and the North West (see the Appendix). A small number of respondents lived outside the UK some of the time and visited periodically for work. Although nearly 20% ($n = 126$) of respondents were based in London and 14% ($n = 92$) in the South East, 38% of respondents ($n = 236$) indicated that they worked in Greater London and a quarter ($n = 154$) in the South East, amongst other locations. Whilst sex workers travelled from across the UK to Greater London, there was also a degree of mobility between regions, for example, across the North East, North West and Yorkshire and the Humber.

As can be seen from the chart in the Appendix, some survey respondents worked in more than one geographical area, which may also relate to touring/travelling being facilitated by the Internet. Some interview participants stated that they travelled for work regularly, either for day appointments across their region of residence and/or to other regions, or staying in hotels or renting a property for work in the UK or other countries for a longer period. For example, Alice (46, a migrant independent sex worker) toured to other regions '*at least one week a month, sometimes two*'. Some independent sex workers would travel to another area and work intensively over a short length of time to build up some capital. Kisses noted that she travelled to other locations when she needed to boost her income:

> …if it's gonna be a case of a bill isn't gonna be paid, I'll be like, crap I need some money. So I'll try and make enough money to see me through for a couple of months, really. So I don't have that for a couple of months, then when I get back in that position, I'll be like, oh god, and I go out again. It's more like that for me. (Kisses, 32, independent sex worker/escort and webcam worker also providing BDSM services)

Amy commented that she had toured regularly in order to balance short bursts of work with time off for other pursuits:

> Well I used to work two weeks away out of every month, and then when I was at home I would barely work at all. So it would be like flat out one week, a week at home, flat out another week somewhere. And I went, well, all over the place [in the UK and also other countries]. (Amy, 43, independent sex worker/escort)

The Internet was seen by research participants to have facilitated not only communication with clients but also online transfer of payments such as advance funding for travel or hotel costs. Access to the Internet is particularly important for sex workers who tour regularly, as it enables them to update their profile to include temporary locations, access marketing sites and make appointments. As Amy remarked, with online directories: '... *with the advertising, you can move your site. Because it's not a physical space, you can change the postcode and move your ad to, you know, anywhere you want in a matter of seconds*'. There has been some discussion recently in the media concerning police activities around 'pop-up brothels', which appear to be based on evidence of temporary renting of properties used for sex work, with services being advertised via the Internet in much the way described by interview participants.[3] What is not clear from these reports, however, is whether these properties are used by independent sex workers who tour the UK, and who may or may not base themselves for a short term with other sex workers, or whether they are indicative of activity organised by third parties. The discourse of modern slavery in the UK sometimes conflates voluntary participation in the sex industry by migrant sex workers with human trafficking, and assumptions may be made about the status of migrant workers in the sex industry, some of whom travel independently for work (Agustín 2007; Mai 2009).

Other interview participants preferred not to tour, because the travelling could be tiring and being in a new location could be problematic, as even with access to alerts from safety and warning schemes, workers needed to familiarise themselves with the area and client base, and thus there were additional safety concerns. As Jill (53, webcam worker and independent sex worker/escort) observed, she had tried touring in the past and: '*It was scary in a way because I didn't know the town, didn't know the people that were coming. So no, I stick locally*'. There were also additional expenses to factor into financial calculations. Ben commented that, whilst some male sex workers also tour for work:

> …tours. Don't like them. I think they're an absolute waste of time and they annoy me. You've got to rack in as many clients as you can in a day. … the reason is, I've got a fantastic in-call premises in a very discreet part of town on a nice street which clients like to come to, right? And I've got my overheads here, my bills and my electricity bill and all that crap, and council tax, but when you go away on a tour, you've got to stay somewhere half decent because they don't wanna turn up on an industrial park in a Travel Lodge. So you've got to be reasonably city centre, reasonably off [a main road or motorway]. You're spending £90 a night just for the hotel, then you've got your travelling expenses, then you've got to keep yourself while you're there, and you've got to keep yourself at home. You've still got to pay your bills at home. You've got to make, if you're gonna do a three-day tour, you've got to get £500 worth of clients through that door before you'll make any money. You might as well just stop at home. (Ben, 43, independent escort and massage provider)

The relatively high cost of hotel rooms and also the additional security procedures in some hotels which mean that visitors may need a key card to use the lifts might also be a reason why some sex workers prefer short-term renting of an apartment for work.

Working Sectors and Patterns of Work

It is difficult to treat Internet-based sex workers as one homogeneous group, as many do different forms of direct and indirect sex work, as described in Chap. 2. Online sex work includes services delivered over the Internet, such as commercial webcam sex, where an individual gives an erotic performance for payment, or 'a pro-domme who skypes with a client for some set exchange value' (Jones 2015a, p. 560). It also relates to the way in which the Internet is used by direct sex workers

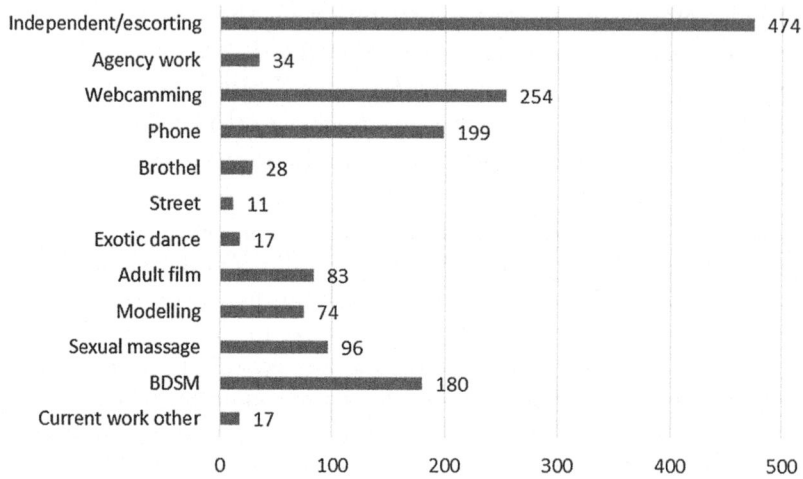

Fig. 3.2 Types of work undertaken. N = 641. *Note* Multiple response so percentages add up to more than 100

to market their services, communicate with and screen clients, and arrange appointments (Ray 2007; Cunningham and Kendall 2011). The Internet has enabled sex workers to network with and support one another online, including not only escorts but also fetish workers, erotic dancers and workers in other sectors, although these forums often tend to be populated primarily by what Ray (2007) and Bernstein (2007b) term 'middle-class' sex workers.

As Fig. 3.2 shows, whilst a majority of BtG survey respondents worked in independent sex work/escorting,[4] a substantial proportion also worked in webcamming.

The majority of respondents ($n = 615$) worked in what can be categorised as independent indoor sectors, that is, independent sex workers/escorts, webcam workers, providers of sexual massage or BDSM services.

There was some difference according to gender: For example, whilst the majority of respondents of all genders worked in independent sex work/escorting, a higher proportion of women than men worked in webcamming, whereas the reverse was true of sexual massage. A small number of both men and women were involved in street work. As

Bimbi (2007) has observed in relation to male sex workers, the Internet is used by all social classes, and access is facilitated by the availability of Internet cafés. Thus, whilst escorts tend to use the Internet for their work, street workers may also make use of digital technologies to make contact with clients. Mac, an interview participant, also noted the value of the Internet for sex workers who did not have their own base, or who were more mobile:

> Well when you're online at least then, say like you're out an about and – a customer's trying to getting in touch with ya, at least he can contact you directly. But whereas when … they're just parking up in a street waiting for you, you don't know they're waiting for you, so at least with the internet you get a bleep on your phone an you know you're required to work. (Mac, 25, independent sex worker/escort also providing BDSM services)

There were also age differences across working sectors amongst survey respondents, with independent sex workers/escorts generally displaying an older age profile than webcammers. For example, 67.6% of those working in webcamming ($n = 171$) were aged 34 and below, compared with 54.6% ($n = 258$) of those in independent sex work/escorting. Conversely, 45.5% ($n = 215$) of independent sex workers/escorts were aged 35 and above, compared with 32.4% ($n = 82$) of workers in webcamming. As Jones (2015a) has suggested, there is a lack of data on the demographic characteristics of sex workers using the Internet, which includes the relative age across different sectors of work. The younger age profile of webcam workers in the survey compared with their independent escorting counterparts may in part be related to the greater emphasis on bodily display in this sector. Nonetheless, there is also age diversity in both sectors.

One of the features of Internet-based sex work is that sex workers may often work in more than one sector and also move between sectors according to need. Flexibility is facilitated by the Internet, where people can fit work around other commitments and change their working patterns according to the amount of business they are receiving from different jobs or other priorities (Sanders et al. 2018). Some survey respondents worked concurrently in several sectors, as also noted in

Chap. 2. The maximum number of sectors worked in (by two respondents) was nine, with the average (mean) number of sectors being two. It was more common, however, for respondents to work in one sector only (41.7% of respondents ($n = 267$), mainly those based in independent sex work/escorting).

Nearly three-fifths of independent sex workers/escorts undertook some other form of sex work: particularly BDSM (27.8%; $n = 132$),[5] webcamming (26.%; $n = 127$) and phone sex work (23.4%; $n = 111$). There was a substantial overlap between webcam and phone workers, with 59.8% ($n = 152$) of webcam workers also undertaking phone sex work. Half ($n = 127$) also worked in independent sex work/escorting.

The greater proportion of respondents (67.7%; $n = 434$) had been doing their current sex work job for 5 years or less. A higher proportion of females than males had been working for more than 5 years (33.9%; $n = 159$, compared with 24.2%; $n = 30$). There was some difference by age: As might be expected, a higher proportion of those aged 35 and above (27.7%; $n = 75$) had been doing their current work for more than 10 years than those in younger age groups (5.2% of those aged 34 and under; $n = 19$).

Nearly three-quarters of respondents (72.1%; $n = 462$) did not share premises with other sex workers. Similar proportions of female and male sex workers shared premises with others at least some of the time. There was no significant age difference amongst those who shared premises. Some interview participants noted that the current legislation in the UK prohibited working with other sex workers, because the working relationship could be interpreted as a brothel. This reflects other studies (e.g. Carline 2011; Pitcher and Wijers 2014) which have noted concerns that independent sex workers risk being criminalised for working collectively.

Use of Other Third Parties

Independent sex workers are self-employed and their position may be compared with that of self-employed lone contractors more generally. For example, independent workers take on all management tasks themselves, or sometimes delegate certain aspects such as web design or accounting to a third party, which may be claimed as a legitimate expense if they are registered as self-employed (Pitcher 2015b). Bruckert and Law (2013) also found that sex workers in their study hired third parties for their specialist skills such as marketing and photography. Nonetheless, in many countries, third parties may be vulnerable to prosecution under the criminal law, which is partly based on assumptions that third parties are inherently exploitative (NSWP 2017).

Most survey respondents did not pay for services to assist with their sex work business. Of those who did, at least some of the time, the main services were accountant (26.5%; $n = 170$) of respondents, with sex workers across all sectors, including the street-based workers, paying for this service. Sex workers who were registered as self-employed would sometimes employ an accountant to complete their annual tax return. Other services included photographer (31.2%; $n = 200$ of respondents, again spread also across all sectors) and web designer (15.7%; $n = 101$ of respondents, reflected across most sectors). Interview participants who used these services commented that they wanted to present a professional image:

> I have a very professional, very polished website, designed for me by a webmaster who I pay to do that. I have professional photographs taken of myself.... The text is very professional. I, I aim myself to be professional, not to look like an amateur. So the pictures don't look like I've taken them with my phone. It's all very slick. (Jane, 40, providing BDSM services)

Sometimes participants were personally acquainted with IT professionals, who would help them to design their website. Third parties were also recruited through word of mouth, for example, through sex worker networking sites. This helped to avoid the possibility of exploitation. For example, Gemma (28, independent sex worker/escort) commented that *'anyone that says they want to take your photo is normally just people just wanting to have a perv and you know, then you've got to trust that person with your photos on their end'*. The potential for sexual or commercial exploitation of sex workers by third parties has also been noted by Pitcher (2015b). Chapter 4 further discusses the risks associated with the use of the Internet by sex workers and steps they take to protect their privacy online.

Hours of Work and Earnings

People may make cost-benefit decisions to work in the sex industry, particularly in independent sex work, because the potential earnings enable them to work fewer hours for higher earnings (Pitcher 2015b). The flexibility of the work and shorter hours may also enable them to fit sex work around other commitments, such as another job or study (Roberts et al. 2007; Scambler 2007). A large proportion of survey respondents only worked up to 10 h per week providing services to clients, but this also has to be balanced against the additional administrative and other work involved, which is largely unpaid (see Fig. 3.3). Whilst not everyone who worked 10 h or fewer per week providing services to clients

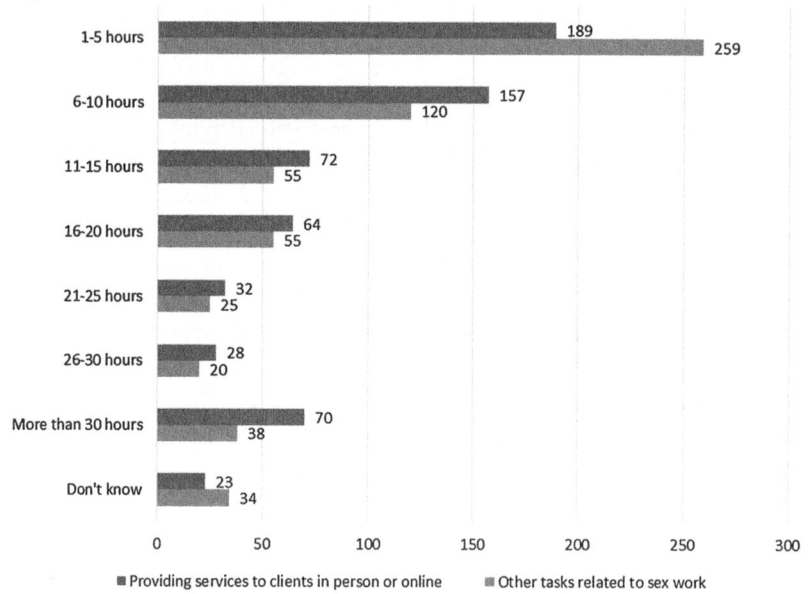

Fig. 3.3 Average hours worked per week. $N = 641$

spent an equivalent amount doing other tasks, 36% ($n = 233$) of all participants worked no more than 20 h per week in total.

Three-quarters ($n = 139$) of independent sex workers/escorts, who worked in no other sex work jobs, and 36% ($n = 26$) of webcam and/or phone sex workers, who worked in no other sex industry sector, spent 10 h or fewer per week on client services. A further 30.6% ($n = 22$) of exclusive webcam/phone workers spent 11–20 h on client services.

There were also some differences in working hours according to age. More than two-thirds of respondents aged 45 and above (67.4%; $n = 64$) worked 10 h or fewer per week on client services. In comparison, 59% of 35–44 year-olds ($n = 98$), 55.1% of those aged 24 or under ($n = 70$) and 50.5% of 24–35 year-olds ($n = 112$) worked 10 h or fewer. This suggests, as Sanders (2007) and Pitcher (2015b) have also noted, that sex workers in older age groups may reduce their hours in preparation for retirement.

Average earnings were not substantial for many, with just over half the sample having gross annual earnings of less than £20,000 (see Table 3.1). Earnings largely corresponded to working hours, with substantially higher proportions of respondents working up to 10 h per week in the lower income brackets (e.g. 54.8% ($n = 171$)

Table 3.1 Average gross annual income from sex work (before any deductions including taxes)

Annual income	No	%
Less than £5000	148	23.1
£5000–9999	83	12.9
£10,000–19,999	102	15.9
£20,000–29,999	77	12.0
£30,000–39,999	40	6.2
£40,000–49,999	38	5.9
£50,000–59,999	29	4.5
£60,000–69,999	8	1.2
£70,000–79,999	9	1.4
£80,000–89,999	7	1.1
£100,000 or more	12	1.9
Prefer not to say	86	13.4
Missing	2	0.3
Total	**641**	**100.0**

earning below £9,999 per annum and a further 30.4% ($n = 95$) earning between £10,000–29,999).

Whilst nearly 17% ($n = 78$) of female respondents earned less than £5,000 annually, nearly 41% ($n = 50$) of male respondents were in this category. Although there were similar proportions of males and females earning £5,000–9999, the proportion of males compared with females earning between £10,000 and 29,999 was significantly smaller. Whilst 14.5% ($n = 58$) of females earned £50,000 or more annually, only 5.5% ($n = 6$) of males were in this earnings bracket.

Comparatively more males than females worked 10 h or fewer per week providing services to clients (nearly 67% ($n = 80$) of males compared with just over half ($n = 233$) of females). To a large extent, this accounted for the lower earnings of male sex workers. Even when controlling for working hours, however, a slightly higher proportion of female sex workers earned more than their male counterparts (70.4% ($n = 145$) of females working 10 h or fewer on client services earned below £20,000 per annum, compared with 77.9% ($n = 60$) of males working equivalent hours). It has been suggested elsewhere (Rosetta 2009) that male escorts are paid less per hour than their female counterparts, which might be an additional factor relating to the slight discrepancy in earnings between male and female sex workers using the Internet. We did not ask participants about their hourly rates in the BtG sex worker survey, however, in part because the qualitative interviews highlighted the difficulties in collecting robust information on this sensitive subject.

There were also some variations by sector: Whilst the earnings for independent sex workers/escorts not working in other sex industry sectors were similar to those for the sample as a whole, nearly 71% ($n = 53$) of those working solely in technology-mediated indirect sex work (webcam/phone workers) earned less than £20,000 per annum. Whilst lower earnings for independent sex workers/escorts are largely accounted for by the lower number of hours worked (92.6%; $n = 87$ of this group earning less than £20,000 annually were working 10 h or fewer per week providing client services), nearly 59% ($n = 30$) of exclusive webcam/phone workers within this earnings category were working more than 10 h per week providing client services.

3 Characteristics and Working Practices of Online Sex Workers

This variation in earnings by sector may also in part relate to the way in which independent sex workers/escorts are paid compared with their webcam counterparts. Independent escorts are paid by the hour and tend to have higher rates than those working in other indoor sectors, such as brothels. In Pitcher's (2014) study, hourly rates for independent sex workers varied between £90 to more than £300. In contrast, chat and cam workers interviewed for the BtG study tended to be paid per minute, with rates varying between 50p–£3 per minute. For those undertaking webcam work through online directories or agencies, a proportion of earnings is also deducted by third parties, as noted in Chap. 2. For example, Sophie (28, webcam worker and independent escort) noted that she could be charged from a third to more than half her earnings, depending on the site she used. There are also variations according to the type of work within this sector: For example, Paris observed that paid group chat was more lucrative as each client is charged:

> Group chat is when multiple men come in the room at any one time. So that's where you really make your money. So if you're doing something, say for example I had a session, I'll give a session, a mixed streaming session where I'm doing strap-on play and I have four guys in a room with me, watching, and that was like these four guys paying £2.00 a minute, so if you do the maths there, that's £16 a minute…. That's where you make your money. That's where … you can command money. (Paris, 33, webcam worker also providing BDSM services)

However, Anna commented that some intermediaries charge more for group chat, which can reduce earnings, so for her, it was more beneficial to go into a private session. Webcam workers may also need to put in additional free time online in order to attract clients into paid group or private showings, which may also account for the different earnings compared with confirmed face-to-face appointments for independent direct sex workers. Anna noted that with escorting:

> …if I get one booking, it's one hour's work. So it's one hour, it's not twelve hours behind a webcam and, at the end of that hour, I know I've

made money. Whereas webcamming, I can sit there for ten hours and not make, you know, not even the minimum wage of a normal job. (Anna, 23, webcam worker and independent sex worker/escort)

Hourly rates within sectors also vary and workers in certain niche markets may charge more. For instance, Jill (53, BBW (big beautiful woman) working in both independent escort and webcam sectors) observed that she charged a higher per minute rate in webcam work than regular webcam workers. Some workers may offer a discount to certain clients. Hannah noted that her prices varied according to the circumstances of her clients:

> I have like a sliding scale when it comes to what money I take. You know, a lot of, a lot of my clients are old-age pensioners, so I give them really generous discount. So a lot of it is almost like a friendship as well in terms of helping, we help each other out. (Hannah, 34, webcam worker also providing BDSM services)

As also discussed in Chap. 2, Internet-based sex workers may have opportunities to supplement their earnings from activities linked to their direct or indirect sex work. For example, some interview participants earned additional income on some sites, by charging for pictures, including photos of certain body parts, selling personal items especially clothing for fetishists or selling erotic stories.

Interview participants noted that earnings could also fluctuate, not only for independent escorts but also for webcam workers, as the number of clients and working hours was not consistent. Nonetheless, earnings are not the only factor relating to job satisfaction and for the hours worked by participants, the income compared favourably with other jobs, even for those whose earnings were not that high:

> Somebody once turned round to me … a client, and said – I used to charge £40 for half an hour, I charge £50 for half an hour now, but I used to charge £40 – he said to me, "Oh, what are you doing these £40 gigs for?" And I said (laughs), "Well, you know these £40 gigs? If I do five of them in a week, that's £200. That's more than working in [a local supermarket] for the week." (Ben, 43, independent escort and massage provider)

Role of the Internet in Working Practices

The Internet appeared to play a large part in improving working practices, for example, in relation to accessing clients, control over working conditions, organisation and independence, as well as safety for many (Fig. 3.4). Slightly fewer respondents saw the Internet as giving access to sources of support, and this may be an area for further investigation. Similar proportions of British and migrant respondents agreed that the Internet gave access to support, indicating that the Internet is a useful source of networking for migrant workers as well as those of British nationality.

Despite the Internet being viewed largely as a positive development for working conditions, in terms of quality of working life and control over working conditions, there were also some disadvantages. Nearly two-thirds ($n = 411$) felt that the Internet had increased the time they spent managing their work, so there was some trade-off between relative autonomy and working hours. Pitcher (2015b) also found that independent self-employed sex workers had to spend a considerable amount of time marketing their services, including spending time on chat boards and other correspondence. Nonetheless, this could also increase their job satisfaction. Survey respondents in the BtG study also had safety concerns about digital technologies, particularly in terms of the potential for hacking data, stalking and being outed. Almost three-fifths of respondents ($n = 376$) had concerns about their identity being revealed to family or friends (for further details see Chap. 4).

Nearly two-thirds of survey respondents ($n = 419$) tended to or strongly agreed that they would not do sex work without the Internet. This related particularly to exclusive webcam/phone workers, with 90.5% ($n = 67$) tending to or strongly agreeing with this statement, but also to two-thirds of independent sex workers/escorts who did not work in any other sex industry sector ($n = 131$). The significant proportion responding in the affirmative to this statement also related to the fact that more than two-thirds of respondents had worked in their current job for 5 years or fewer: A smaller proportion of those who had been working for more than 5 years (55%; $n = 113$) agreed to this statement, compared with nearly 72% ($n = 306$) of those who had worked for 5 years or fewer.

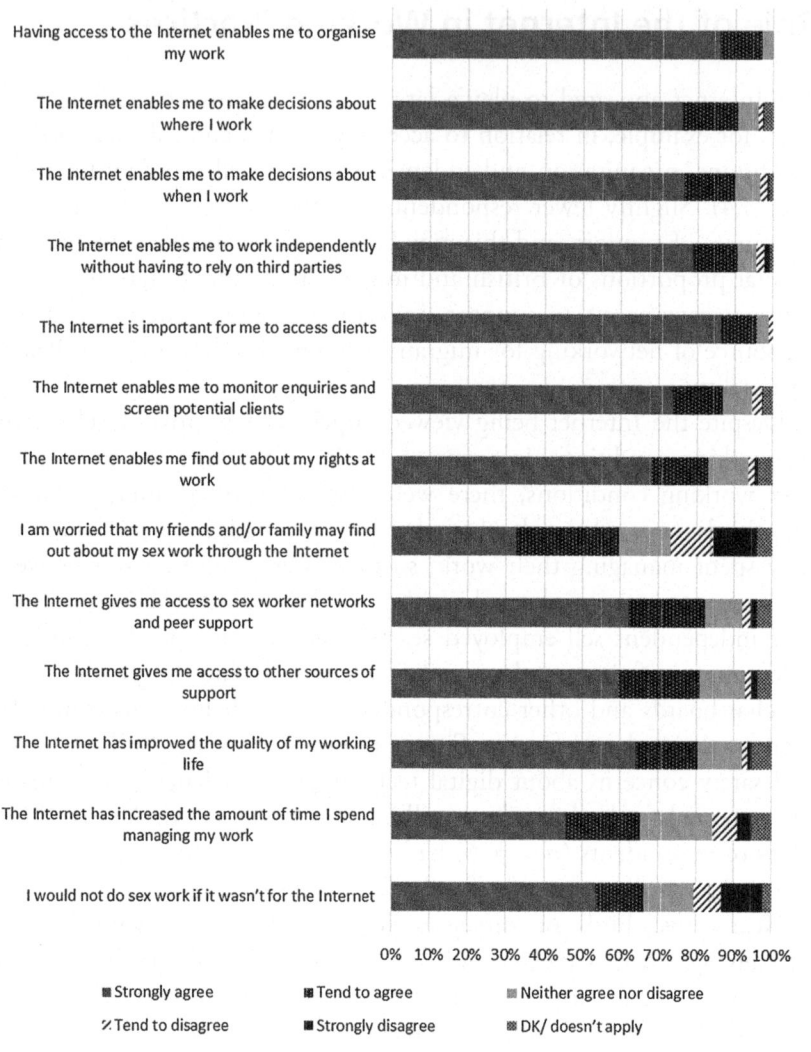

Fig. 3.4 To what extent do you agree or disagree with the following statements about the use of the Internet and digital technologies for your work? $N = 641$

The Internet was clearly vital for webcamming and also instant messaging, as confirmed by interview participants. For participants who worked across different sectors, they might have phone sex work and/or escorting to fall back on if the software failed, although the Internet has also become an essential medium for effective advertising. The Internet was seen to have changed the way sex workers market themselves. For those who had been working in the sex industry for some time, advertising their services via the Internet was cheaper and more immediately effective than previous newspaper advertising and had become more essential as other marketing avenues had become closed off or reduced. As Marcus commented:

> …there's a lot of pressure on me to market myself and to stand out against all the competition. That said … the great thing about the internet is you can put an ad on in five minutes. If you put a print ad on, it can, you can wait a month for it to get published. So with the internet it's instant. And when I very first started doing the sexual massage after my break, I didn't have a website because I'd let that go, didn't have time to put a print press ad, so I all I did was put one advert on Gumtree, which was very cryptic because you're not allowed to put sexual adverts on there. I, I remember very clearly I put it on on the Monday and by the Thursday I'd seen ten clients. (Marcus, 42, independent sex worker/escort and sexual massage provider).

Having access to digital technologies enabled participants to build up their own business, which may not have been an option previously. Interview participants also emphasised the independence having access to the Internet gave them, for contacting clients, advertising and screening potential clients, as also discussed in Chap. 4. Hannah commented that:

> Oh, I think it's … fundamentally important. I wouldn't have a working life if it wasn't for the internet. Yeah, I think, I sort of think back about attitudes around, like, how I thought about sex work and getting into it, and I think I've always had in my head, like when I see like a dominatrix on telly, I've always thought, well I could do that, but how would you get into it? It just seems ridiculous. … But having met people and realising that you network and you promote yourself independently, using the internet, means I have access to advice. I know how to keep myself safe and I get to have access to clients. And I'm also able to interact with them and vet them so that, you know, I can continue working in a, in a good, healthy, relatively stress-free way. (Hannah, 34, webcam worker also providing BDSM services)

As she also noted, the Internet had opened up more diverse avenues of work, and digital technologies enabled people to be more flexible with working times according to the need for income:

> …the technology is there in your phone, in your tablet, and it's all taken care of by a third party. So I can, you know, I can work whenever I feel like it and wherever I am. And, you know, when, when you're a bit skint, thirty quid can feed your family for a few days, so I can log on for half an hour and I can make that money and, within a week, it will be in my account. (Hannah, 34, webcam worker also providing BDSM services)

One of the effects of increased use of the Internet for marketing services, as noted by Marcus earlier, was that it could be more difficult to stand out from other sex workers. Milena observed that not only had the number of sex workers advertising online increased, but there was more diversity in the range of services offered:

> As I said, there's quite a lot of girls based here. … In my area, quite, quite a lot. And I mean two years ago when I started it wasn't that much. For some reason there has been, whoa, let's go there. And since the last 12 months, I would say, there has been like an – is the word influx? … Of like increase of like sex workers. It's ridiculous. And they cover now everything. We do couples, we do like MMF, FFM, like all sorts and you like sit over there and you think, "How can I make myself more interesting?" So you need to be really, really out there. (Milena, 32, independent sex worker/escort also providing BDSM services)

Although participants were aware of the need to market services effectively, the immediacy of the Internet might bring safety concerns if there was less time to screen potential clients. Marcus spoke of the importance of being aware of how the wording of adverts and website design might appeal to certain clients and the need to target advertising accordingly:

> …the thing about the internet is you have to word your website or your advert in a particular way in order to attract a certain kind of client. So I'm looking for people who are gonna treat me with respect, who are

3 Characteristics and Working Practices of Online Sex Workers

> prepared to pay a little bit more. I'm slightly above the average monetary-wise per hour, only a little bit, but you get a better quality of client that way. And when I say better quality of client, I mean your safety … is more protected if you word your ad in a specific way. And I've only learned that the hard way, you know, because a lot of sex ads can be sleazy, very hardcore. And I think there's a place for that, it's not necessarily a problem, but I've noticed that when I have kind of copied that kind of marketing I've had what I could call poor quality clients where they've haggled the price, they've not been respectful, I've not enjoyed myself. Because the thing about my job is I absolutely love it, and if I'm not enjoying myself with a client, I'm doing something wrong. So I had to up my marketing in that to make sure that I have the right client for me and that they have the right worker for them. (Marcus, 42, independent sex worker and sexual massage provider)

Participants generally enjoyed the challenge that building an online business gave them, however, and were able to make most of the opportunities the Internet gave them for marketing, negotiation with clients and establishing contractual expectations. For instance, Amber linked her website to her profile on social media and also provided advice to clients on her expectations of appropriate behaviour and how to be a 'good client':

> Being able to work online and technology is absolutely essential to me. There is no way that I could or that I probably would work without it, I don't think. Yeah, I mean it's a space between the client and me. It's an area where I can display all the information and, you know, it's a negotiation in between what a client expects and what I'm willing to deliver. And that's laid out on my website. You know, I have an FAQ and etiquette guide. And I use social media, which is linked to my website. As I said – my branding is really strong. I link to a Twitter feed in my website. And yeah, my tweets, they're – you know, they're all kind of cued. They're all kind of autocued. Th– you know, I'm aware they're client-facing so they're always very cheery and very optimistic but, you know, kind of helpful. They're like tips on how to be a good client, you know, that kind of thing. Not so overtly, as I've just kind of said, but yeah, I find that really useful. (Amber, 25, independent sex worker/escort also providing massage and BDSM services)

Although interview participants sometimes used third party sites, they relied less on individual third parties (such as taxi drivers and hotel concierges) to promote their services, as they could create their own website or put an advertisement on one or more sites. This could also help them feel more secure from police harassment:

> Whereas now what you've more got is everybody on the internet because you can't be arrested for it. You can't be policed and tracked down and, like, you don't fear that reprisal of the law banging at your door and harassment. You know, they've got to do a lot more research to come and track you down. (Paris, 33, webcam worker also providing BDSM services)

Whilst some migrants to the UK might work in brothels/managed premises initially for security and companionship, this option may not be available in some geographical areas, particularly for male sex workers. For migrant workers new to the UK who wish to work independently, the Internet has proved vital for networking to find out about rights and establishing contacts:

> …I think, especially in this country, I mean it's very important. It's like – how do you say – vital? … Yeah. Er, without it, I don't think I could do sex working in [Scottish city], as a migrant sex worker especially. Er, in [my home country] I was doing street work because I didn't have a place and sometimes I was using my friends' houses, but mostly like I was in the streets. And it's easier because like when you know the country, you know, you know your rights and you're a citizen of the country so I think I was a bit less scared. Um, but here, like even indoors, like since it's safer than outdoors actually, but being a migrant gives me the this worry, this extra worry, um, because I know like if the police found out, like will [I] be treated as same I'm sure like maybe a British person, or I think like that…. So without the internet, like I couldn't do street work either in [Scottish city], so for me like it's the only way kind of. I mean also because there's no male brothels that I can, you know, consider to join. So it's pretty much it. (Ruzgar, 27, independent sex worker/escort)

Whilst there may be barriers to independent self-employed work for some migrant workers, as discussed earlier, for others this may be the only feasible and relatively safe working sector.

Conclusions

Online sex work is a growing sector which until fairly recently has been less explored than other working sectors in the sex industry. Whilst the BtG study contributes to the literature, showing diversity in online sex work, differential working patterns and indicating the way in which demographic characteristics of sex workers using the Internet for their work may differ from those of workers in other sectors, it also emphasises where there continue to be gaps in information. These relate particularly to a more comprehensive mapping of the UK sex industry and the overlap between different forms of working practices, more detailed exploration of the sexuality of online sex workers and their clients and the need for research targeted specifically at migrant sex workers in online sectors.

The BtG study has provided important new information on earnings and working hours of sex workers in different sectors, including independent sex work/escorting and webcam work. It also explores earnings differentials not only according to work type and working patterns but also gender and age. This chapter demonstrates the importance of the Internet for marketing, networking and safety, as well as providing an essential medium for certain types of online sex work. It also emphasises the role the Internet has played in enabling independent sex work, with less reliance on third parties for advertising and facilitating contact between workers and clients, unless sex workers themselves opt to employ professional services for their business.

The BtG study highlights the importance of touring for some independent sex workers and the need to make clear distinctions between touring for individual business purposes and the discourse of modern slavery which conflates independent travel for work with trafficking and coercion.

Notes

1. Note: Because of small numbers, it was necessary to merge male–female and female–male transgender respondents; and non-binary and intersex survey respondents.
2. Because of low numbers in other gender categories, comparisons could not be drawn in many instances.
3. www.telegraph.co.uk/news/2017/02/05/30-pop-brothels-open-week-swindon-police-warn-foreign-prostitutes/, accessed 10 May 2017.
4. This was the term used in the survey questionnaire, after extensive consultation with sex workers, as some people who work in direct independent sex work prefer this term to that of 'escort'.
5. Note that BDSM refers both to in-person services, but may also apply to technologically mediated services, for example, in the case of financial domination.

References

Agustín, L.M. 2006. The Conundrum of women's agency: Migrations and the sex industry. In *Sex work now*, ed. R. Campbell, and M. O'Neill. Willan: Cullompton.

Agustín, L.M. 2007. *Sex at the margins: Migration, labour markets and the rescue industry*. London: Zed Books.

Bernstein, E. 2007a. *Temporarily yours: Intimacy, authenticity and the commerce of sex*. Chicago: University of Chicago Press.

Bernstein, E. 2007b. Sex work for the middle classes. *Sexualities* 10 (4): 473–488.

Bimbi, D.S. 2007. Male prostitution: Pathology, paradigms, and progress in research. *Journal of Homosexuality* 53 (1): 7–35.

Bruckert, C. and T. Law. 2013. *Beyond pimps, procurers and parasites: Mapping third parties in the incall/outcall sex industry*. Ottawa: University of Ottawa, Available at http://www.powerottawa.ca/ManagementResearch.pdf. Accessed 22 March 2017.

Carline, A. 2011. Criminal justice, extreme pornography and prostitution: Protecting women or promoting morality? *Sexualities* 14 (3): 312–333.

Cole, R.E., E. Jeffreys, and J. Fawkes. 2015. The best parties happen under the bus: The impact of lesbian institutions on queer sex workers in Australia. In *Queer sex work*, ed. M. Laing, K. Pilcher, and N. Smith. London: Routledge.

Comte, J. 2014. Decriminalization of sex work: Feminist discourses in light of research. *Sexuality and Culture* 18 (1): 196–217.

Cunningham, S., and T.D. Kendall. 2011. Prostitution 2.0: The changing face of sex work. *Journal of Urban Economics* 69 (3): 273–287.

Gaffney, J. 2007. A coordinated prostitution strategy and response to paying the price—But what about the men? *Community Safety Journal* 6 (1): 27–33.

Global Network of Sex Work Projects. NSWP, 2017. The decriminalisation of third parties. Policy brief. Edinburgh: NSWP. Available at http://www.nswp.org/resource/policy-brief-the-decriminalisation-third-parties. Accessed 22 March 2017.

Jeal, N., and C. Salisbury. 2007. Health needs and service use of parlour-based prostitutes compared with street-based prostitutes: A cross-sectional survey. *BJOG: An International Journal of Obstetrics and Gynaecology* 114 (7): 875–881.

Jenkins, S. 2009. Beyond gender: An examination of exploitation in sex work. PhD thesis, April, Keele University.

Jones, A. 2015a. Sex work in a digital era. *Sociology Compass* 9 (7): 558–570.

Jones, A. 2015b. For black models scroll down: Web-cam modeling and the racialization of erotic labor. *Sexuality and Culture* 19 (4): 776–799.

Koken, J.A. 2012. Independent female escort's strategies for coping with sex work related stigma. *Sexuality and Culture* 16 (3): 209–229.

Koken, J.A., D. Bimbi, J.T. Parsons, and P.N. Halkitis. 2004. The experience of stigma in the lives of male Internet escorts. *Journal of Psychology and Human Sexuality* 16 (1): 13–32.

Lee-Gonyea, J.A., T. Castle and N.E. Gonyea. 2009. Laid to order: Male escorts advertising on the Internet. *Deviant Behavior* 30: 321–348.

Mai, N. 2009. *Migrant workers in the UK sex industry—Final policy-relevant report*. ESRC final project report. London: London Metropolitan University.

Murphy, A., and S. Venkatesh. 2006. Vice careers: The changing contours of sex work in New York city. *Qualitative Sociology* 29: 129–154.

Office for National Statistics. 2016. *Sexual identity, UK: Experimental official statistics on sexual identity in the UK in 2015 by region, sex, age, marital status, ethnicity and NS-SEC*. London: ONS.

Perkins, R., and F. Lovejoy. 2007. *Call girls: Private sex workers in Australia*. Crawley: University of Western Australia Press.

Pilcher, K. 2012. Dancing for women: Subverting heteronormativity in a lesbian erotic dance space? *Sexualities* 15 (5/6): 521–537.

Pitcher, J. 2014. Diversity in sexual labour: An occupational study of indoor sex work in great Britain. PhD thesis, November, University of Loughborough. https://dspace.lboro.ac.uk/2134/16739.

Pitcher, J. 2015a. Direct sex work in great Britain: Reflecting diversity. *Graduate Journal of Social Sciences* 11 (2): 76–100.

Pitcher, J. 2015b. Sex work and modes of self-employment in the informal economy: Diverse business practices and constraints to effective working. *Social Policy and Society* 14 (1): 113–123.

Pitcher, J., and M. Wijers. 2014. The impact of different regulatory models on the labour conditions, safety and welfare of indoor-based sex workers. *Criminology and Criminal Justice* 14 (5): 549–564.

Ray, A. 2007. Sex on the open market: Sex workers harness the power of the Internet. In *C'lick me: A netporn studies reader*, ed. K. Jacobs, M. Janssen, and M. Pasquinelli. Amsterdam: Institute of Network Cultures.

Roberts, R., S. Bergström, and D. La Rooy. 2007. Commentary: UK students and sex work: Current knowledge and research issues. *Journal of Community and Applied Social Psychology* 17 (1): 141–146.

Rosetta, A. 2009. *Whatever she wants: True confessions of a male escort*. Reading: Ebury Press.

Sanders, T. 2005. *Sex work. A risky business*. Cullompton: Willan.

Sanders, T. 2006. Behind the personal ads: The indoor sex markets in Britain. In *Sex work now*, ed. R. Campbell, and M. O'Neill. Willan: Cullompton.

Sanders, T. 2007. Becoming an ex-sex worker: Making transitions out of a Deviant career. *Feminist Criminology* 2 (1): 1–22.

Sanders, T., L. Connelly, and L. J. King. 2016. On Our Own Terms: The Working Conditions of Internet-Based Sex Workers in the UK. *Sociological Research Online* 21 (4): 15, http://www.socresonline.org.uk/21/4/15.html.

Sanders, T., M. O'Neill, and J. Pitcher. 2018. *Prostitution: Sex work, policy and politics*. London: Sage.

Scambler, G. 2007. Sex work stigma: Opportunist migrants in London. *Sociology* 41 (6): 1079–1096.

Sharp, K., and S. Earle. 2003. Cyberpunters and cyberwhores: Prostitution on the Internet. In *Dot cons. crime, deviance and identity on the Internet*, ed. Y. Jewkes. Willan: Cullompton.

Smith, N., and S. Kingston. 2015. Policy-relevant report: Statistics on sex work in the UK. Birmingham: University of Birmingham and Lancaster: University of Lancaster.

TAMPEP International Foundation. 2007. *TAMPEP VII final report: Activity report*. Amsterdam: TAMPEP International Foundation.

Walby, K. 2012. *Touching encounters: Sex, work, & male-for-male internet escorting*. Chicago: University of Chicago Press.

Whowell, M., and J. Gaffney. 2009. Male sex work in the UK: Forms, practice and policy implications. In *Regulating sex for sale: Prostitution policy reform in the UK*, ed. J. Phoenix. Bristol: Policy Press.

4

Crimes and Safety in the Online Sex Industry

Abstract In this chapter, we explore the types of crimes that Internet-based sex workers' experience, and the rise of new forms of crimes such as harassment, stalking, unwanted contact and misuse of information and images. We assess the role of the Internet and technology in safety strategies, uncovering some of the ways in which technology benefits sex workers' ability to keep safe, but at the same time, technology generates some additional risks. Alongside crime, risks in this sector relate to additional privacy issues for online working—something which is an everyday concern for many working through online spaces. This research adds significantly to the literature on crime and safety in the online sector and also highlights how current UK laws can restrict rather than promote safety for people working in this sector.

Keywords Crimes against sex workers · Persistent or repeated unwanted contact · Threatening or harassing texts, calls or emails
Verbal abuse · Non-payment · Reporting to the police · Safety strategies
Online safety · Privacy · Online community

Introduction

Whilst there is a considerable body of research examining sex workers experiences of violent and other crime (Deering et al. 2014; Kinnell 2008) relatively little is known specifically about internet-based sex workers experiences and how they manage risks (Moorman and Harrison 2016). Whilst a preceding study of a smaller number of UK respondents ($n = 241$) by Sanders, Connelly and Jarvis-King (2016) considered types of crimes experienced by internet-based sex workers, the current Beyond the Gaze study offers some comparative findings. In this chapter, we explore what crimes sex workers working online experience, and the rise of new forms of crimes. We assess the role of the internet and technology in safety strategies, uncovering some of the ways in which technology benefits sex workers' ability to keep safe, but at the same time technology generates some additional risks. Alongside crime, risks in this sector relate to additional privacy issues for online working—something which is an everyday concern for many working through online spaces.

Crimes Experienced by Online Sex Workers

Most respondents (80.8%; $n = 518$) in our survey had experienced at least one form of crime in the past 5 years. Four hundred respondents (62.4%) had experienced at least one of the crimes listed in Table 4.1 in the past 12 months. Of these, 21.5% ($n = 86$) had experienced only one type of crime and 21.8% ($n = 87$) had experienced two types of crime in the past year. The average (mean) number of different types of crime experienced in the past 12 months was three. Overall, the actual level of violence reported by respondents in the last 5 years and last year was relatively low. The following respondents reported NOT experiencing these crimes in the past 5 years in their working capacity:

- sexual assault 77.8% ($n = 499$)
- threat of violence 72.9% ($n = 467$)
- physical assault 84.4% ($n = 541$)

4 Crimes and Safety in the Online Sex Industry

Table 4.1 Have you experienced any of the following crimes or incidents in the past 5 years and/or past 12 months in your current sex work job?

	Yes, in the past 5 years		Yes, in the past 12 months		Not experienced in the past 5 years	
	No.	Percentage (%)	No.	Percentage	No.	Percentage (%)
Threatening or harassing texts, calls or emails	360	56.2	233	36.3	274	42.7
Verbal abuse	315	49.1	199	31.0	313	48.8
Persistent or repeated unwanted contact or attempts to contact you through email, text or social media	417	65.1	292	45.6	219	34.2
Repeated unwanted contacts or attempts to contact in person, or persistent following or being watched	186	29.0	105	16.4	441	68.8
Physical assault	83	12.9	32	5.0	541	84.4
Sexual assault (including rape or removal of condom without consent)	125	19.5	49	7.6	499	77.8
Threats of violence	160	25.0	81	12.6	467	72.9
Theft or robbery	86	13.4	31	4.8	531	82.8
Non-payment or attempting to underpay for services	345	53.8	212	33.1	286	44.6
Burglary (e.g. unlawful entry to your property with intent to steal, do damage or inflict bodily harm)	36	5.6	11	1.7	587	91.6
Use of your personal information or account details to obtain money or buy goods/services without your consent	49	7.6	23	3.6	573	89.4
Other	35	5.5	19	3.0	269	42.0

$N = 641$

In the last year 7.6% ($n = 49$) had experienced sexual assault, 5% ($n = 32$) had been physically assaulted, 12.6% (n-81) had been threatened with violence. Levels of violent crime experienced by online sex workers in our survey were lower than those reported by sex workers in other sectors in key UK research studies. For example, Church et al. (2001) in a study comparing experiences of female indoor parlour and street sex workers in three UK cities found 81% of street workers reported ever experiencing violence (with 50% in the last 6 months), compared to 48% and 26% respectively of indoor sex workers. Yet we found relatively high levels of online harassment, non-payment and verbal abuse, but lower incidences of violence and other crimes (see Table 4.1). More respondents had the following experiences than did not:

- persistent or repeated unwanted contact or attempts to contact though email, text or social media
- threatening or harassing texts, calls or emails
- verbal abuse
- Non-payment of attempts to underpay for services

The most commonly experienced types of crime experienced were similar to those found by Sanders et al. (2016), in their survey of online sex workers, the most commonly reported crimes experienced in their study were, threatening or harassing texts, calls and email (36%) and verbal abuse (30%). Yet these were reported at a higher level by people in our survey 56.2% ($n = 360$) and 49.1% ($n = 315$) respectively having experienced these in the past 5 years. Persistent or repeated unwanted contact or attempts to contact through email, text or social media were the most commonly experienced crimes experienced in our study, reported by 65.1% ($n = 417$), this was not a category included by Sanders et al. (2016).

In most of the crime categories there were no major gender differences. But notably more female than male respondents had received threatening texts, calls or emails in the past 5 years (58.4%; $n = 274$ compared with 46.8%; $n = 58$) and repeated unwanted email contacts in the past five years (66.1%; $n = 310$ and 55.6%; $n = 69$). Female sex workers were also somewhat more likely than male respondents to have received these unwanted contacts in the past 12 months (46.3%; $n = 217$ compared with 37.1%; $n = 46$). While the numbers are relatively small, a higher proportion of female than male respondents had experienced physical assault over the past 5 years (14.5%; $n = 68$, compared with 8.1%; $n = 10$): and also sexual assault (20%; $n = 94$ compared with 12.9%; $n = 16$). For male sex workers, the online sector has been identified as safer than street work (Aggleton and Parker 2015; Koken et al. 2010) offering a *'less stigmatizing environment with lower risk of violence, with a higher level of safety'* (Argeneto et al. 2016, p. 9). Yet some studies illustrate that violent crime can be an issue for online male sex workers, Gaffney and Jamell (2010) in a survey of $n = 107$ UK based male and transgender sex workers, the majority of whom were male and males who contacted customers via online methods reported 20% had ever been *'forced to have anal or oral sex without consent'* by a client.

In our survey there were also some differences according to respondents' age. For example, a lower proportion of survey respondents aged 45 and above had experienced threatening texts, calls or emails in the past 5 years or 12 months than younger age groups (47.5%; $n = 48$ compared with an average across all age groups of 56.3% over the past 5 years and 24.8%; $n = 25$ compared with an average of 36.5% over the past 12 months). Similarly, proportions of the same age group had experienced somewhat lower than average non-payment over the same time periods (47.5%; $n = 48$ compared with an average of 54% over five years and 25.7%; $n = 26$ compared with an overall average of 33.2%). While the numbers were low and thus caution should be exercised in interpreting the findings, respondents aged 45 and above reported somewhat below average levels of physical assault (7.9%; $n = 8$, compared with an average across all ages of 13%) and sexual assault (13.9%; $n = 14$ compared with an overall average of 19.6%) over the past 5 years. Threats of violence were also lower for this age group over the same time period (13.9%; $n = 14$, compared with an average of 25%). Levels of theft or robbery over the past 5 years for this group, however, were slightly above average (16.8%; $n = 17$, compared with an average of 13.5%). These differences according to age may be related to factors such as experience or working patterns, but this is an area that may be investigated further.

It is important to compare independent sex workers/escorts who worked exclusively in that sector with technology-mediated indirect sex workers (TMIs such as webcammers) who worked in no other sectors (with no in person contact and hence reduced opportunity for certain crime types) while the numbers are relatively small for TMI workers, it does appear that there are some minor differences in relation to the types of crime experienced. For example, while 60.2% ($n = 118$) of those who worked exclusively as independent sex workers/escorts had encountered threatening texts, calls or emails in the past 5 years, 55.1% ($n = 27$) of TMI-only workers had experienced this. On the other hand, percentages were not dissimilar for verbal abuse, and relatively high proportions of both groups had experienced non-payment or attempts to underpay (55.6%; $n = 109$ of independent sex workers 53.3%; $n = 40$ of TMI-only workers). Although the numbers are very small and thus caution should be exercised here, TMI workers appeared less likely to have experienced any form of violence in their work, we might speculate that there is an association here with the fact that this group of workers does not have in-person contact with clients in their normal work routine. In interviews webcam and phone workers described how they felt safer because they didn't have face-to-face contact with clients.

How do these statistics on sex worker crimes fit with the context of violent crimes in the general population? The Crime Survey for England and Wales (CSEW, Office of National Statistics 2016a) reports that men were more likely than women to be a victim of violence in the year ending March 2015. When considering intimate personal violence, including stalking, however, women were more likely than men to have experienced this form of violence (Office of National Statistics 2016b). There were also age variations, with women and men in the younger age groups more likely to have encountered intimate violence. In relation to workplace violence, the survey found that 1.3% of women and 1.5% of men had been victims of violence at work during the year prior to their interview (Health and Safety Executive 2016). The levels of violence varied per occupation, however, and certain groups, particularly those in protective service occupations, such as police officers, but also those in health and personal service occupations, had much higher than average levels of assault (Health and Safety Executive 2016). While the methods of data collection were different and thus caution should be exercised in interpreting the findings, comparing the proportions of sex workers in Table 4.1 who had experienced violence at work such as physical assault, theft or robbery in the past 12 months, with the occupations in the CSEW deemed to be at higher risk of violence, the incidence of physical violence encountered by sex workers was broadly similar to that experienced by health and social care associate professionals and slightly lower than that for protective service occupations.[1]

Building on the research of Sanders et al. (2016) our research highlights that whilst levels of violent crime in the online sector appear to be relatively low (although not insignificant) particularly compared to the street sector, the growth of the online sector to be the largest sector of the UK sex industry has seen a shift in crime trends within sex work. Salient within this change is the prevalence of crimes which are digitally enabled, particularly those which exploit sex workers concerns about privacy and identity violations. This shift to digitally enabled cybercrime needs also to be understood in the context of the criminalisation of sex work, and the methods of control through which sex work is governed (Graham 2017).

Reporting Crime

A key finding of the research on sex work and violence is that incidents of violent and other crime committed against sex workers are seriously under-reported to police (Kinnell 2006, 2008; Boff 2012; Church et al. 2001). Similarly, crimes amongst online sex workers went unreported: only 114 (23%) out of 496 respondents stated that they had ever reported incidents to the police, proportionately more female than male respondents (25.4%; $n = 93$ compared with 16.5%; $n = 15$). Only 33.1% ($n = 212$) of respondents stated they were *'quite'* or *'very likely'* to report incidents to the police in future, whereas 39% ($n = 250$) felt they were '*quite*' or '*very unlikely*' to report incidents. Indicators of limited confidence to report to the police were found by Sanders et al. (2016) with nearly half of their respondents (49%) either confident or very unconfident that the police would take their crime seriously.

Of those in the BtG survey who had ever reported incidents, 46.5% ($n = 53$) were quite or very satisfied with how the complaint had been handled by the police, 14% neither satisfied nor dissatisfied and 39.5% ($n = 45$) quite or very dissatisfied. Mixed experiences of reporting to the police were also identified amongst interview participants who had reported incidents to the police. Here in cases of outing which included harassment, threats and 'doxing' (posting personal details online) the varied experience of police responses is illustrated:

> He posted my pictures all over the Internet, making Facebook pages up in my real name…to try to control me…I went to the police. In the end of the police raided his house and took all his computer equipment away and destroyed it. But they were very good. (*Alex, 53 escort*)
>
> My crazy neighbour found me on cam, he reported me to my landlord… he contacted a journalist about what I did and I had a reporter outside the house for two days… he put a letter through one of my other neighbours doors complaining about me…it's horrendous. I passed that onto the police and they were like, it's not a criminal matter. I was furious. (*Jane, 29, female webcammer*)

Such experiences of reporting harassment to the police must be understood in the wider UK context where police and Crown Prosecution Service responses to reports of harassment and stalking specifically have been identified as inadequate, with HM Inspectorate of Constabulary's (HMIC) and HM Crown Prosecution Service Inspectorate (HMCPSI) (2017) reporting serious failings in these responses with crimes not recorded, not taken seriously and poorly investigated. Existing studies identify a range of reasons for under-reporting of crime to the police by sex workers including: a lack of confidence in the police; a belief the police will take no action (Penfold et al. 2004), will not give a sympathetic reaction and will judge sex workers (Kinnell 2006), a belief that they will not be taken seriously and that crimes will be treated as an occupational hazard and personal experiences of previous unsatisfactory response from the police (O'Neill and Campbell 2002). Anxiety about arrest and prosecution, of themselves or others they work with, in the case of people working in premises where more than one person works (which could be defined as brothels within law) is a prominent reason (Boff 2012; Pitcher 2015) and distrust of authorities and fear of deportation for migrants, particularly those who are undocumented or have irregular legal status (Mai 2009). Bryce et al. (2015) highlighted specific issues for male sex workers whose experiences are rarely recognised in policy and service provision with few agencies including the police with initiatives to remove barriers to reporting and access victim support. Reasons for not reporting amongst indoor sex workers identified have also included: embarrassment, not thinking the incident was serious enough, believing no one would care, fear of losing their job (for parlour and agency workers) (O'Doherty 2011).

Even in a context within which sex workers are working legally in terms of laws on sex work, as is often the case for online sex workers in the UK, our research found that for many online sex workers numerous barriers remain to reporting crime to the police. Some key reasons revealed in interviews for under-reporting amongst people working in the online sector included: not wanting anyone to know about their sex working, fear that reporting meant the police and other authorities would become aware of their sex work, a fear that reporting may lead to legal action against them including if they worked with other sex workers or for some migrants immigration related action, that reporting may lead to family, friends and others becoming aware that they are sex working and a view that the crime was not serious enough to report or would not be taken seriously.

Sex Worker Safety, Online and Digital Technology

Jones (2015) notes that the internet has made a difference to sex workers' working practices and conditions—including enhancing safety procedures. The internet plays an important part in safety at work—for three quarters of survey respondents it was reported as very important (47.1%; $n = 302$) or quite important (28.1%; $n = 180$) (Fig. 4.1). Only 6.5% ($n = 42$) thought it was not very or not at all important (Fig. 4.1).

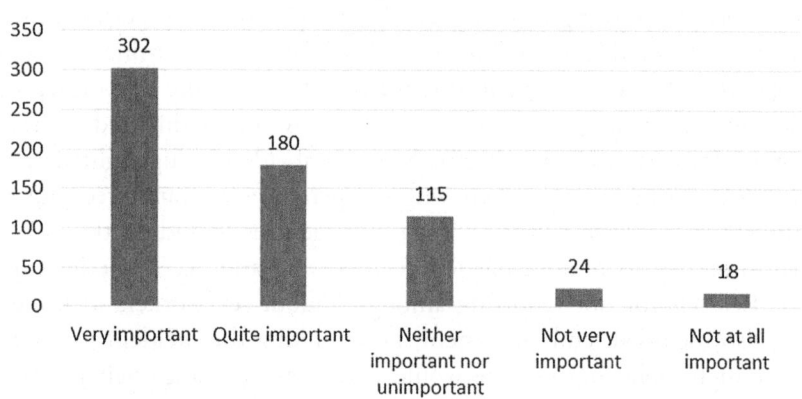

Fig. 4.1 Internet's role in safety strategies. $N = 641$

Comments from respondents across all genders in relation to the role of the Internet in safety were largely positive, seeing it as providing opportunities for a range of safety measures. The main benefits to safety from using the internet related to being able to screen potential clients, to network with others and to access information about safety, with sharing info about potentially dangerous clients being central to such networking. These benefits are illustrated by survey respondents:

> I worked for many years pre-internet and was very isolated. I was clueless about safety, enforcing boundaries and even the basics of how to manage client interactions. Now, I can chat things through online—from the smallest worries to major safety issues. When I do in calls in hotels, my screening is fairly lax but I'm popping in and out of Facebook all day so my friends have tabs on me. Services like NUM are vital and undoubtedly prevent women meeting dangerous clients. Also, Platform 47 for things like hotel info—not all hotels are workable and it's terrifying to imagine being busted by the police. (Female independent sex worker, aged 35–44)

> Allows me to screen clients, communicate with other workers, update my buddy on my whereabouts and safety, etc. (Non-binary independent sex worker, webcammer and worker in other indoor sectors, aged 18–24)

The Internet is an excellent means of gathering information and conducting research. There are many sites that offer tips on safety and 'do's and don't's' which is invaluable to me. (Male sex worker, aged 18–24)

Whilst people identified the safety benefits some also voiced concerns, particularly in relation to the risk of being identified, being outed, stalked, having data stolen for instance and concerns that sites used are vulnerable to hacking (leading to loss of credits/income). The following comments from survey respondents identify this twin track nature of the Internet for sex workers as both risky yet an enabler of safety:

To look up/screen clients, to check numbers, to check addresses. I worry about family or police finding out about my work through my advertising though (*Non-binary independent sex worker, webcammer and BDSM provider, aged 18–24*)

It [the internet] only helps with sharing dodgy client information. The internet is accessible by all and I risk upsetting and causing distress to my family and friends if they ever found out. (Male independent sex worker, aged 25–34)

The Internet was seen as important in enhancing safety, through access to peer networks and forums, ugly mugs reporting and warning services and access to information and functions to support client screening.

Online Blended Safety Strategies

We have established that the internet and mobile technology was very important amongst sex workers in our study for enhancing safety (see Fig. 4.2) but the adoption of online safety methods had not extinguished 'traditional' offline methods. Moorman and Harrison (2016) noted online sex workers combine online screening with safety techniques used in other sectors such as street and brothel settings. Sex workers in our survey were asked which methods they used to enhance their safety, selecting from a list of fourteen mechanisms. Our research evidences that online sex workers generally blend online and off-line methods in multi layered safety strategies.

The majority of workers put in place specific safety methods, although 87 (13.6%) stated they did not take any of the precautions listed. This does not mean these workers had not considered safety: some participants in the 'other' response indicated response options were 'not relevant' to them and the most commonly mentioned reason for this was that they did not work in a sex work job where they had in person direct contact with customers, for example webcamming, phone or live messaging sex chat. Also for others a range of factors were identified as barriers for putting in place safety methods for example concerns about identity and data protection, sex workers may be reluctant to sign up to forums or safety schemes or informally network with other sex workers.

In the survey the most frequently identified safety strategy was a non-digital precaution, *'avoiding drugs or alcohol at work'*, with 64.2% ($n = 357$) using this method. This has been a working practice seen as a safety measure for many years by sex workers, it is understood as a means of being alert to the behaviour of customers during bookings and better able to respond quickly and manage difficult situations (Sanders 2005a; Day 2007). The third most used method by survey participants was also a non-online tech one: nearly 41.7% ($n = 246$) saw only or mostly regular clients as a safety method. This has long been a risk reduction screening strategy employed by some sex workers in all sectors (Sanders 2005a).

Screening Potential Clients

As shown in Fig. 4.2 screening potential clients was the second most utilised method identified in the survey, 44.2% ($n = 246$) identified that they carried out screening. Also in a separate question 72.1% ($n = 462$) strongly agreed that *'the internet enabled them to monitor enquiries and screen potential clients'*, with a further 12.9% ($n = 83$) tending to agree, only 2.8% ($n = 18$) tended to disagree or strongly disagreed. O'Doherty (2011, p. 11) defines screening as: *'a conscious and proactive strategy employed prior to meeting clients. It is a strategy employed by some agencies and many independent sex workers'*. Interview

4 Crimes and Safety in the Online Sex Industry

What methods do you use to enhance your safety when you are working?

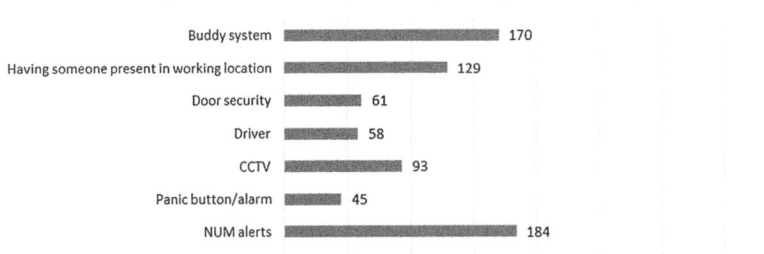

Fig. 4.2 Enhancing safety at work. N = 641. Multiple response question, so percentages add up to more than 100

data showed the screening of potential clients was employed by the large majority of sex workers, particularly those offering in person services, many of whom described adopting multi layered screening strategies. Ray (2007, p. 57) noted that screening existed before the internet but *'the Internet has streamlined the process'* and described how independent sex workers who worked through the internet rely on several different forms of screening and that there were different levels of screening from worker to worker. Argento et al. (2016, p. 1) compared male street and internet based workers and found online workers had increased capacity to screen potential customers and reported that the *'Internet can provide greater opportunities to negotiate terms of sex work and enhanced screening using webcams, reducing risks of violence, stigma'*.

We found that screening encompassed a range of practices with workers often mixing online/digital and offline approaches, with mobile and smart phone technology being embedded in many sex workers working practices. We list some of the main screening strategies here:

- Not make a booking without having spoken to a customer over the phone: this was important for the majority of sex workers offering in person services.
- Not making a booking if a withheld number is used.
- Not accepting bookings with people whom they had previously blocked.
- Googling clients to find out more about them including utilizing professional networking sites and searching social media.
- Checking the IP address of a potential client.
- Checking forums/ugly mugs schemes/advertising platforms to see if the individual has any warnings or negative feedback about their behavior.
- Using number check applications lined to sex industry warning schemes and generic online and phone number ID and blocking applications.
- Checking own personal 'bad clients'/ugly mugs list, data base or stored numbers.
- Taking credit card details or deposit into an account so there was digital footprint related to bank details was a method connected to safety for some sex workers.

Most people had a screening regime which incorporated a range of methods. Hausbeck et al. (2017) in their research with independent US online escorts found they use a range of screening techniques, with a '*screening progression*' with the three aims of: avoiding law enforcement officers (in the US context where it is a crime to sell sexual services), avoid time wasters and for safety. Hausbeck et al. (2017) report a range of methods including gut instinct, online research, references from other sex workers about customers, apps and tools in the ID verification industry which has grown up in the US. The following comments from BtG survey participants illustrate similar screening methods and demonstrate the importance placed by many on pre-appointment screening involving online or telephone research, communication and negotiation:

> I check the IP addresses of people I don't know for fraud and scams and check phone numbers if they have been reported through Google. (Male independent sex worker, aged 35–44)

I am able to make decisions about the clients I see prior to the meeting. Thus I can expect to see profiles/previous meeting reviews/pictures/information on their personal details. (Male independent sex worker, masseur and model, aged 25–34)

I Google people on Facebook with their phone number keep excel sheet database, always inform friends where I currently work we exchange information about clients on the regular basis. (Female independent sex worker/escort, aged 25–34)

Ugly Mugs Warnings: Sharing Information About Dangerous People and Timewasters

Noted as our main partner in the Introduction to this book, the National Ugly Mugs (NUM) scheme was introduced to link local ugly mugs schemes and to complement existing peer-led and industry based warning boards aiming to alert sex workers, increase reporting of crimes against sex workers, aid investigations and prevent crime against sex workers. In terms of how respondents used the alerts and warnings, a third (33.1%; $n = 181$) used National Ugly Mugs (NUM). Ugly Mugs Ireland (UMI) like NUM provides an online platform where sex workers can report incidents and receive alerts: 1.6% ($n = 9$) used Ugly Mugs Ireland Alerts (reflecting a small proportion on respondents working in Northern Ireland or the Republic of Ireland). Such platforms are proving an important resource for online sex workers (particularly those providing in person services) and our qualitative data showed that sex workers who were members valued them:

> It's safer. They have a lot of built-in systems now in a way of protecting escorts that are out there…especially with the introduction of the Ugly Mugs system, because you know, it's so easy to put a report through and then anybody who's registered, like I get emails on a regular basis for things that have happened all over the North West. (*Cait, 52, independent sex worker working in webcam and other services*)

> I'm on Ugly Mugs. I check quite frequently because then that way at least if a name pops up on Ugly Mugs and I've had a customer of the same whatsit book, then I know that hang on a minute there's summat dodgy here. (*Mac, 52, independent sex worker providing domination and BDSM services*)
>
> I'm using National Ugly Mugs. So sometimes they are like emailing if there's a, you know, killer on the loose or something like that. I also reported like a couple of phone numbers in the past to National Ugly Mugs. (*Ruzgar, 27, independent sex worker*)

Many sex workers interviewed used at least either a third-party reporting scheme which issued warning alerts, sex worker peer forums with warning systems or other sex worker networking groups who shared information about people of concern amongst members. With many using more than one sources of warnings or information about problematic customers:

> I'm signed up to the National Ugly Mugs scheme and I read the messages that they send out. I also check the warning section on the forum (Platform 47), just to see if there's anybody in my area that has been causing problems. (*Heather, 31, independent sex worker*)
>
> I'm subscribed to Ugly Mugs, and obviously, I check (Platform 47) as well, yeah… Platform 47 saved me from one dodgy client. (*Kay, 48, independent sex worker*)

For female escorts this combination of NUM and Platform 47's warnings were very commonly combined with smaller private sex worker groups that shared warnings:

> I run numbers through Platform 47 and also I am actually part of a private Facebook group which kind of developed from Twitter. We kind of moved onto Facebook a bit to be more organised and we're like a secret group. We like to post numbers on there and stuff. (*Amber, 25, independent sex worker also working in massage, domination and other services*)

Our survey and interviews also flagged the importance of online spaces which as part of wider functionality provided warning systems and information sharing about timewasters, problematic customers including those who commit crimes against sex workers, which have been developed for specific groups of sex workers. For example, several male sex workers identified Platform 47 a forum specifically for UK based gay and bisexual male escorts and masseurs and it's board on scams and people of concern as a space to check as part of screening: *'We get, like, warnings about dodgy clients … So I think that it's useful for guys that are coming into it and don't have much experience'. (Boyd, 32, independent sex worker working in massage, domination, webcam and other services).* BDSM service providers identified specific forums run by and for people working in their sector as important for alerting and sharing about problematic people.

The warnings functions of forums were particularly mentioned by interview participants who provided in person services as they had to meet and manager customers face to face. The safety functions of sex worker forums and other peer networks facilitated by social media primarily sharing information about potential customers, reporting and warnings about individuals of concern and accessing safety buddies were flagged by many sex workers in our study and are now central for sex workers in safety practices.

Number Checkers

There are a number of online platforms which offer number checking schemes. This is the case for NUM and UMI which as well as issuing warning alerts have a number checker function. 25.9% ($n = 144$) of participants in the BTG sex work survey used a phone number checker and findings from qualitative interviews showed that a section of workers utilise such tools, with several number checker services identified. The majority who mentioned the number checkers identified using ones linked to sex work industry safety schemes, forums and sex worker advertising platforms:

> Well, firstly you've got your instant number checker on Ugly Mugs. I don't use that very often. I use the one from (Platform 17), just because it's easier. If I get an enquiry that I just find it suspicious—sometimes you just get a feeling in this kind of work—I would run the number there. I would also run it through Google. Sometimes that comes up on other sites where the number's been flagged for whatever reason. (*Marcus, 42, independent sex worker also providing massage services*)

Some participants also specified using a caller ID and number block application designed for any person to use regardless of profession to identify who is using a particular telephone number. One female escort explains their perception of how it operates:

> There's an app … What they do is mass data collection for whoever has the app… it's a search app. If you put a number… into it, it will come up with the names that other people have listed for that number… I find it really useful. So most of the time my screening will mean that I have a full name for clients, but I track their number…as well. So that's really useful for safety. (*Amber, 25, independent sex worker also providing massage, domination and other services*)

Feedback, References and Registration Digital Footprint

US research (Cunningham and Kendall 2011; Cunningham and De Angelo 2017) has highlighted the importance of client references or '*letters of reference*' for safety. These are references sex workers obtain from other sex workers about customers, these can be accessed via specific online websites. In the UK, no parallel system has emerged which has systematised and formalised references to the same degree, although notes/ratings by other sex workers as part of some advertising platforms functions, warning boards and third party ugly mugs reporting schemes allow sex workers to access some information about those individuals who have been reported as problematic in some way. One escort participant described how her membership of a private Facebook group allowed her to 'ask for references':

We'll like people who will see the same clients and ask for references. Like sometimes I ask for references, like who else have you seen? And then I'll contact that person and be like, 'What was he like?' So I don't tend to use the boards so much, but I think that I'm probably unusual in that I'm not so representative. (*Amber, 25, independent sex worker also providing massage, domination and other services*)

A survey respondent who worked in modelling and other sex work jobs asked for references for others they would be working with in the modelling setting: '*References for photographers, riggers, other models before I work with anyone*' (*Non-binary webcamming, phone sex work, modelling and BDSM, aged 25–34*)

Survey respondents and several interviewees referred to a function which had been offered by a market leading adult services website (Platform 1), this had enabled the sex worker to leave a comment about the customer (not accessible to customers) following a booking. Other sex workers could then read the comment to ascertain if there were any matters of concern such as they: had been time waster, were aggressive, too pushy, or tried to remove a condom. All of these behaviours were identified by many sex workers as warning signs for further problematic behaviour and crime. Hence these comments had been used to inform whether they accepted a booking, the removal of this feature was mentioned by several participants in interviews and survey comments:

My main concern with (Platform 1) is their removal of the 'notes' feature, where workers could share comments relating to client's behaviour. This was a really vital safety feature as it could be used to say things that couldn't be mentioned in public feedback, like violent or boundary pushing behaviour. (*Female independent escort providing webcamming, BDSM services and also working in the adult film industry/porn, aged 35–44*)

Indeed, sex workers also identified working and contacting clients via platforms which required customers to register as important for safety because of the digital footprint customer left: '*any client who contacts me through Platform 1 is traceable, to an extent, having to provide at least basic information to sign up and also an IP can be tracked*' (*45–54, male,* independent sex worker providing webcamming, phone sex work and also works in the adult film industry/porn). Whilst some sex workers stressed that whilst such registration systems were not infallible with the possibility of false or proxy registrations, they did see them as one level which required possibly traceable customers information and hence may act as one deterrent. Internet based sex workers in the UK are working within existing online search functions, forums and warnings schemes to piece together information about customers as part of their screening procedures.

Buddying Systems

In our survey just under one third, 30.6% ($n = 170$) reported that they used a buddy system. In survey comments and interviews sex workers described varying buddying arrangements utilised, these were used to a greater extent by escorts and BDSM workers and others who provided in person services. Some workers buddied with other sex workers, friends or a partner not working in the sector:

> Ringing a friend to 'check in' and 'check out' when I am doing an outcall. I check in, in front of the client so they are aware that someone knows where I am'. (*18–24, male, independent escorting, webcamming, sexual massage and BDSM services*)

> Telling friends where I am, messaging them and sending them my address. Also meeting clients in public prior to any in call. (*18–24, female, independent sex work/escorting*)

Mobile phone technology SMS, other messaging applications and social media have provided options and networks for buddying arrangements and can make checking in with buddies a safety measure which is cheaper and easy:

> I actually found my personal Twitter account really useful in terms of safety. If I'm doing like an overnight outcall, I can check in with someone on Twitter in a different time zone. I don't sleep on overnights, I basically

see it as a night shift. You know, sometimes it can be a new client, and I don't want to text my partner at like three AM. But if I can just drop a private message to someone who has all the details of where I am and just be like hey, you know, everything's great. I'll text you at ten am you know, stuff like that, which is really useful. (*Amber, 25, independent sex worker also providing massage, domination and other services*)

The Presence of Others, Third Parties and Environmental Features

Research has illustrated how the organisation of indoor sex work can reduce risk relative to street sex work (Sanders and Campbell 2007; Scott et al. 2005; O'Doherty 2011; Kinnell 2006, 2008). These studies which have tended to be based on samples of indoor sex work particularly in managed massage parlour/brothel environments have identified the presence and role of others including fellow sex workers, receptionists and security staff who can deter and intervene, as important safety measures which can deter crime. In our sample of predominantly independent online sex workers these were also strategies employed. Just under a quarter 23.2% ($n = 129$) identified having someone present in their working locations as a method for enhancing safety strategy. 11% ($n = 61$) used door staff and 10.4% (58) used a driver (see Fig. 4.2) which was identified as a specific safety strategy by some of those who did outcalls as independents of agency workers.

It is also salient to note that in a survey question about services sex workers pay for to assist with their sex work business only 7.3% ($n = 47$) engaged a driver with a further 6.9 ($n = 44$) doing so sometimes, 3.9% ($n = 25$) engaged security and a further 3.3 ($n = 21$) sometimes, 4.2% ($n = 27$) engaged a receptionist/maid a further 2.5% ($n = 16$) doing so sometimes. This shows that for a small group, having third party support is part of their business model. Yet it is well documented that organising work to include other sex workers and third parties also raises problems regarding the law for sex workers. Sex workers sharing premises with other sex workers, working collectively, risk being charged with assisting in or managing a brothel. As do receptionists, maids and other third parties who work with more than one sex worker (Pitcher 2014). Our survey found that whilst just under a quarter of sex workers shared premises with other sex workers, most did not. But strikingly in relation to safety, when survey participants were asked what change they felt could most improve sex worker safety, allowing sex workers to work together was the most frequently identified measure.

A Note on Gender, Migrancy and Safety

Whilst our survey found no substantial gender differences in safety methods, there were some notable exceptions: female respondent were more likely than male respondents to use sex worker forums for safety (33.5%; $n = 157$ compared with 16.1%; $n = 20$ for men). Females were also using NUM alerts to a greater level compared to males (30.7%; $n = 144$ compared with 19.4%; $n = 24$). In interviews, some male sex workers noted how they perceived some established sex worker forums and NUM to carry more warnings about incidents involving perpetrators who target female sex workers and hence were not as relevant to them. Women were more likely than males in the survey to share information informally (37.1%; $n = 174$ compared to 28.2%; $n = 35$). Women were also more likely to have someone present in working location (21.5%; $n = 101$ compared with 13.7%; $n = 17$).

There is a need to further explore internet based migrant sex workers' specific experiences of crime and use of safety strategies. This imperative is highlighted by research exploring changing patterns in the sex industry which shows migrants are now a significant cohort in the UK sex industry and in some sectors and geographical areas of the UK for example London, form a majority (Mai 2017). Also there has been a large increase in the number of migrants amongst sex workers who are the victim of work related murder (Sanders et al. 2017). Our research only begins to indicate one aspect of the structural, intersectional disadvantage experienced by migrant sex workers in the online sector and how limited cultural and linguistic capital can restrict access to certain safety information and resources. In our survey in open text related to safety a migrant sex worker commented: '*I am Romanian so find it hard to read or find info that may be useful'* (*female, independent escort*). Migrants with limited English skills are placed at a disadvantage in relation to various safety resources for example some warning schemes and boards do not provide waring alerts in other languages (Platt et al. 2011). It may be difficult to navigate websites and applications, and to utilise safety information without translation functions, this may make some migrants more dependent on third parties for such information.

Protecting Privacy

For most sex workers interviewed privacy was intertwined with professional boundary maintenance and safety. Nearly half of respondents overall (48.8%; $n = 313$), and 52.7% ($n = 39$) of webcam/phone only workers, had concerns about their privacy online. A key privacy concern for many survey respondents was that their personal identity would be discovered for example via work accounts or profiles being linked to personal accounts on Facebook, WhatsApp, Twitter and other social media.

> With the increased use of social media and messaging platforms which connect data, it is sometimes worrying that work accounts will be linked to personal accounts. (*Female, independent escorting, aged 25–34*)

Concerns about the security of platforms and the possibility of the hacking of those platforms exposing personal details. Identity theft was a concern as was photographs or video being used by other sex workers or others on platforms online without consent: this included cases where privacy was a concern but also cases where copyright and commercial issues were a concern. Family, friends, neighbours, current and future employers finding out was one of the most prominent concerns expressed: '*Someone from my personal life or an employer will find images of me*' (*Female webcammer, aged 18–24*). '*People like neighbours, landlords finding out, or people I don't want/can't be out to, like my partners family or if I want to apply for a job, my future boss*'. (*Female, independent sex work/escorting providing webcamming and phone sex, aged 25–34*). Family being exposed and placed at risk were a concern and those with children feared how the authorities would respond and what impacts this would have on their dependents:

> I have small children and I live in a rural village. I worry that I'll be outed, or people will report me to child protective services even though my children are never exposed to my phone and cam work, nor are they aware of what I do for a living. (*25–34, female, independent sex work/escorting providing webcamming and phone sex*)

There was concern that people could blackmail them using the threat of outing and exposure as part of blackmail, 'being *found' by a family member. Having a client figure out my identity and use that to harass or blackmail me*' (*Female independent escort, aged 18–24*). Being partially or fully outed itself was a big concern as was the misuse of information (doxing) where personal details and face photos or videos were taken from websites and placed elsewhere for others to view. The potential for online stalking was also an issue of concern, '*That I'll end up with a stalker, my information will be stolen or that people I haven't told will find out*'. (*Female, webcamming, phone sex work and exotic* dancing/stripping, aged 18–24).

These were not just concerns but had been experienced by some, for example over a third stated that information they had put online had been used without their consent 37.4% ($n = 240$) and this proportion rose to 45.9% ($n = 34$) of webcam/phone only workers. These included incidents where commercial benefit had been the motive yet also where malicious identification, doxing and outing had been the motivation:

> Men wanted to avoid paying for my content, and this happens to a lot of sex workers who upload stuff. They find their content on free sharing and torrenting sites. (*35–44, female providing phone sex and BDSM services*)

> Lots of sex sites copy your pictures and profile and add it to make them look like they have more members than they have. I have also had two

male sex workers use my pictures in their profiles. (*Male escort providing phone sex, aged 35–44*)

One guy put a short clip of me giving him a bj up… One guy told me he had filmed our encounter and that he would put it online if I wouldn't sleep with him again, (I didn't) but I have no idea if he did upload it, or even secretly film in the first place. (*Female escort working in a brothel also providing webcam services, aged 25–34*)

Friends at uni found out and shared my escorting profile amongst all my other friends. I was distraught, felt ashamed and upset. (*Male independent escort, aged 25–34*)

For the large majority of participants in BtG survey and interviews, maintaining privacy was a daily work related concern. Research has highlighted how stigma has a number of detrimental impacts on sex workers, many sex workers are anxious about the implications of their sex work being revealed to people known to them and more widely. For many sex workers this can entail maintaining a 'double' or 'secret' life' which can be stressful (Sanders 2005a; Mai 2009). In our research, many sex workers were managing not being open about their sex work status to a range of individuals in their family, friendship and neighbourhood networks. Others felt that due to stigma associated with sex work, and prejudicial attitudes, other parties such as: future or current employers, educational establishments and other public institutions may be judgemental if their sex work is known, also potential media exposure was also seen as threat. Some sex workers who were open to their family, friendship and wider networks also had specific boundaries that they wished to maintain regarding for example making a separation between work and none working life or personal data sharing. Sex workers were not passive in the face of invasions of privacy. For the majority protecting privacy and identity (generally and online) were primary concerns and hence taking steps to protect privacy was one of the most important work related matters. Sex workers taking part in our survey were asked to identify which steps they took to protect their identity online (see Fig. 4.3).

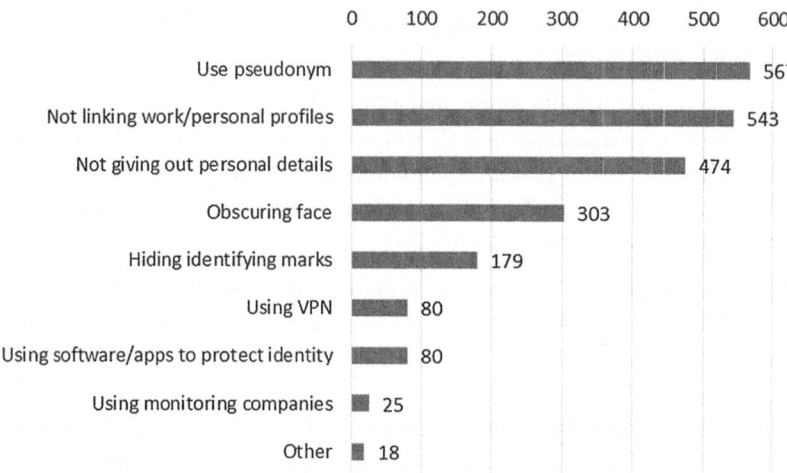

Fig. 4.3 Steps to protect identity online

The most popular measure was using a pseudonym with 91.5% ($n = 567$) respondents doing so, followed by not linking work with personal profiles on online spaces, 87.6% ($n = 543$) took this precaution and 76.5% ($n = 464$) did not give out personal details making this the third most popular precaution. The popularity of the first and third of those practices illustrate how as with safety repertoires many sex workers blended digital and non-digital methods for privacy protection. Obscuring their face in images was used by 48.9% ($n = 303$) and 28.9% said they hid identifying marks. A virtual private network (VPN) was used by 12.9% ($n = 80$) of respondents, these can be used to add security to public and private networks, with the persons IP address (unique address for each computer or device) being replaced with one from the VPN provider. The same percentage used software or applications to protect their identity online, some referred to specific applications and software they used, most commonly phone applications which allowed them to ascertain user ID, spam and block calls from people about whom they have concerns may compromise their privacy:

> Hide my IP, change my images to make them harder for Google to recognise, watermark everything, never use personal details on dmca's.[2] *(Female providing webcamming, phone sex work and modelling services, aged 35–44)*
>
> Seeking out and attempting to eliminate information about me on foreign sites that I do not use. *(Male independent sex work providing services such as: webcamming, exotic dancing/stripping, adult film industry/porn and modelling (glamour/erotic, aged 18–24)*

In interviews and survey responses a key theme of discussion for people who had experienced violations of privacy with personal details or content on line without their consent was the response they had received from websites, forums, social media organisation in cases where they had directly made contact requesting content be taken down or making formal complaints. Responses ranged from requests being swiftly acted upon to those where it had been a lengthy process for action to be taken or the complaint was ignored. Many of those who provided further information about 'other' steps taken illustrated the combination of privacy protection precautions people utilised, including employing online or digital technology or using tech in a particular way consciously to protect privacy: *'Always deleting my browser history.* (*Female independent escort, 25–34*), *'I even used a fake ID, different phone, different sim card, different Skype, separate email, separate web browser (no other searching), deleting cookies hidden on my computer only for this'*. (*Male independent escort, aged 25–34*)

Sex workers for many decades (Sanders 2005a, b) have utilised a physical work appearance different to their non-work appearance and style as one means of identity protection, physical disguise was employed by some online sex workers: *'I wear different wigs/extensions and hair pieces to disguise myself'* (*Transgender male to female escort also providing other services 25–34*). A female escort aged 25–34 explained: *'I blank my face and also wear wigs in the pics and when with clients. Also don't give my number of property out'*. Carefully separating work and personal life on online profiles and social media use was commonplace:

> I also avoid using the same images on my work/personal profiles to protect from reverse image searches. I don't post/tag photos of myself on my personal social media profile and use a (different) pseudonym on there too. (*Non-binary escort also providing webcam, phone sex work, modelling, sexual massage, BDSM services and works in a brothel, aged 25–34*)

Others had purposefully chosen not to engage with social media or certain telecommunications platforms which they felt compromised privacy, this was an issue touched on earlier when reflecting on why some sex workers are wary of social media: '*Don't use any social media at all including Google + whether working or not*'. (*Female independent escort, aged 35–44*). Online working presented new threats to privacy but also new tools for protecting privacy and sex workers provided a number of examples of the dual edge nature of online technology. An escort who routinely used a telephone ID and blocker application as part of her safety repertoire noted how this application could also expose sex workers:

> So you could be speaking to your mum on your phone and someone's listed you, like some client has listed you on there, Wales escort, you know, if your mum looks at that, so that's another one where people have got caught out as well. (*Amber, 25, independent sex worker also providing massage, domination and other services*)

The majority of internet based sex workers in our study took consciously considered actions to protect privacy, many learnt about various online methods for protecting privacy via their own online research and networking with other sex workers. Strategies adopted were shaped by: people's preferences, knowledge, level of digital literacy and access to technology, working methods, circumstances and decision making about how they manage the public/private nature of their sex work in both online and in person relationships and networks. As with safety strategies, sex workers blended online technology approaches with offline practices to protect privacy.

Conclusion

Beyond the Gaze has produced some important insights into the ways in which technologies which shape the organisation and working practices of sex workers have affected the crimes experienced by sex workers. Whilst the experiences of sexual assault and physical violence are relatively small, there are high levels of online crimes reported, resulting in more people experiencing threatening or harassing texts, calls or emails; verbal abuse; persistent or repeated unwanted contact or attempts to contact though email, text or social media, the majority of these incidents are not reported to the police. Digital risks noted were specifically in relation to privacy with anxiety and concern particularly around identity exposure and social media and other forms of outing. To prevent crime and violations of privacy occurring and to optimise safety within the current regulatory framework, several technologies are utilised to enhance safety strategies, primarily assisting workers to screen potential clients. Other key strategies were to network, share and access information about safety through digital sources. Yet we also found that sex workers not only use digital safety and privacy protection methods but blend these online methods with more traditional 'old school' repertoires of precaution as deterrents and protections to keep themselves safe and protect privacy.

BtG's findings about internet based sex workers experiences of crime and safety (for example lower levels of violent crime compared to other sectors, differential risks and strategies for people working in different sex work jobs within the online sector) supports the need to employ and further develop an intersectional framework (Hill-Collins 1990; O'Neill and Campbell 2002; Moorman and Harrison 2016, International Committee on the Rights of Sex Workers in Europe 2014) to make sense of the complex structural, organisational and subjective factors which interact to shape online sex workers experiences of 'risk', crime and safety and more widely, diverse experiences within internet based sex work.

Notes

1. In the past 12 months, 5% of BtG survey respondents reported experiencing physical assault and just under 5% had encountered theft or robbery. While methods of recording crime are different and therefore no exact comparisons can be made, 6% of health and social care associate professionals and more than 9% of those in protective service occupations in the 2015/16 CSEW had experienced violence at work in the past year (HSE 2016, p. 6).
2. This refers to requests made under the US Digital Millennium Copyright Act (implementing two treaties from 1996) to take down online copyright—people can use third party services to get stolen content taken down.

References

Aggleton, P., and R. Parker. 2015. *Men who sell sex: Global perspectives*. New York, NY: Routledge.

Argento, E., M. Taylor, J. Jollimore, S. Taylor, J. Jennex, A. Krusi, and K. Shannon. 2016. The loss of Boystown and transition to online sex work: Strategies and barriers to increase safety among men sex workers and clients of men. *American Journal of Men's Health*: 1–12.

Bar-Johnson, M., and P. Weiss. 2015. A comparison of male sex workers in Prague: Internet escorts versus men who work in specialized bars and clubs. *The Journal of Sex Research* 52 (3): 338–346.

Boff, A. 2012. *Silence on Violence: Improving the safety of women—The policing of off street sex work and sex trafficking in London*. Available at: http://glaconservatives.co.uk/wp-content/uploads/downloads/2012/03/Report-on-the-Safety-of-Sex-Workers-Silence-on-Violence.pdf. Accessed 12 July 2017.

Bryce, A., R. Campbell, J. Pitcher, M. Laing, A. Irving, J. Brandon, K. Swindells, and S. Safrazyan. 2015. Male escorting, safety and national ugly mugs: Queering policy and practice on the reporting of crimes against sex workers. In *Queer sex work*, ed. M. Laing, K. Pilcher, and N. Smith, 245–255. Abingdon: Routledge.

Church, S., M. Henderson, M. Barnard, and G. Hart. 2001. Violence by clients towards female prostitutes in different work settings: Questionnaire survey. *British Medical Journal* 322: 524–525.

Cunningham, S., and T.D. Kendall. 2011. Prostitution 2.0: The changing face of sex work. *Journal of Urban Economics* 69 (3): 273–287.

Cunningham, S., and G. De Angelo. 2017. 'Signals, screens and vertical differentiation: The case of commercial sex work', presented in COST Prospol, displacing sex for sale, 29–31 March. Copenhagen: University of Aalborg.

Deering, K., A. Amin, J. Shoveller, A. Nesbitt, C. Garcia-Moreno, P. Duff, A. Argento, and K. Shannon. 2014. A systematic review of the correlates of violence against sex workers. *American Journal of Public Health* 104 (5): e42–e54.

Day, S. 2007. *On the game: Women and sex work*. London: Pluto Press.

Gaffney, J. and J. Jamell. 2010. Male and trans sex worker needs assessment survey, presented at *Harm Reduction: The Next Generation, 21st IHRA Conference*, 25–29 April 2010, Liverpool Echo Arena.

Graham, L. 2017. Governing sex work through crime: Creating the context for violence and exploitation. *The Journal of Criminal Law* 8 (3): 201–216.

Hausbeck-Korgan, K., A. Nelson, A. Izzo, S. Bessen, and S. Lopez-Embury. 2017. 'Displacing client anonymity: Power sexual politics and safety dynamics in Online Provider Vetting Processes' presented in COST Prospol, displacing sex for sale, 29–31 March. Copenhagen: University of Aalborg.

Health and Safety Executive. 2016. *Violence at work: Findings from the Crime Survey for England and Wales and the Reporting of Injuries, Diseases and Dangerous Occurrences and Regulations*. London: HSE. Available from: http://www.hse.gov.uk/statistics/causinj/violence/index.htm. Downloaded 12 April 2017.

Hill-Collins, P. 1990. *Black feminist thought: Knowledge, consciousness and the politics of empowerment*. London: Routledge.

HM Inspectorate of Constabulary's (HMIC), and HM Crown Prosecution Service Inspectorate (HMCPSI). 2017. *Living in fear: The police and CPS response to harassment and stalking A joint inspection by HMIC and HMCPSI*, HMIC. Available at: http://www.justiceinspectorates.gov.uk/hmic/wp-content/uploads/living-in-fear-the-police-and-cps-response-to-harassment-and-stalking.pdf. Accessed 12 July 2017.

International Committee on the Rights of Sex Workers in Europe. 2014. *Structural violence: Social and institutional oppression experienced by sex workers in Europe*. Amsterdam: ICRSE.

Jones, A. 2015. Sex work in a digital age. *Sociology Compass* 9 (7): 558–570.

Kinnell, H. 2008. *Violence and sex work in Britain*. Cullompton: Willan Publishing.

Kinnell, H. 2006. Murder made easy: The final solution to prostitution? In *Sex work now*, ed. R. Campbell, and M. O'Neill, 141–169. Willan: Cullompton.

Koken, J.A., D.S. Bimbi, and J.T. Parsons. 2010. Male and female escorts: A comparative analysis. In *Sex for sale: Prostitution, pornography, and the sex industry*, 2nd ed., ed. R. Weitzer, 205–232. New York: Routledge.

Mai, N. 2009. *Migrants in the UK Sex Industry: Final policy relevant report*. London: Institute for the Study of European Transformations, London Metropolitan University.

Mai, N. 2017. Sexual humanitarianism: Migration, sex work and trafficking—2016–2020. https://sexualhumanitarianism.wordpress.com/.

Moorman, J.D., and K. Harrison. 2016. Gender, race, and risk: Intersectional risk management in the sale of sex online. *Journal of Sex Research* 53 (7): 816–824.

O'Doherty, T. 2011. Victimization in off-street sex industry work. *Violence Against Women* 17 (7): 1–20.

Office of National Statistics. 2016a. *Overview of violent crime and sexual offences: Findings from analyses based on the year ending March 2015 Crime Survey for England and Wales and crimes recorded by the police covering different aspects of violent crime*. London: ONS.

Office of National Statistics. 2016b. *Intimate personal violence and partner abuse*. London: ONS.

O'Neill, M., and R. Campbell. 2002. *Working together to create change: Walsall prostitution consultation research*. Walsall: Walsall South Health Action Zone/Staffordshire University/Liverpool Hope University.

Penfold, C., G. Hunter, R. Campbell, and L. Barham. 2004. Tackling client violence in female street prostitution: Inter-agency working between outreach agencies and the police. *Policing & Society* 14 (4): 365–379.

Pitcher, J. 2014. Sex work and modes of self-employment in the informal economy: Diverse business practices and constraints to effective working. *Social Policy and Society* 14 (1): 113–123.

Platt, L., P. Grenfell, C. Bonell, S. Creighton, K. Wellings, J. Parry, and T. Rhodes. 2011. Risk of sexually transmitted infections and violence among indoor-working female sex workers in London: The effect of migration from Eastern Europe. *Sexually Transmitted Infections* 87 (5): 377–384.

Ray, A. 2007 [2005]. Sex on the open market: Sex workers harness the power of the internet. In *C'lickme: A netporn studies reader*, ed. K. Jacobs, M.

Janssen, and M. Pasquinelli, pp. 45–68. Amsterdam: Institute of Network Cultures.

Sanders, T. 2005a. *Sex work: A risky business*. Cullompton, Devon: Willan Publishing.

Sanders, T. 2005b. It's just acting: Sex workers. *Strategies for Capitalising on Sexuality', Gender, Work and Organization* 14 (4): 319–342.

Sanders, T., and R. Campbell. 2007. Designing out vulnerability, building in respect: Violence, safety and sex work policy. *British Journal of Sociology* 58 (1): 1–19.

Sanders, T., L. Connelly, and L. Jarvis King. 2016. On our own terms: The working conditions of internet-based sex workers in the UK. *Sociological Research Online* 21 (4): 15.

Sanders, T., S. Cunningham, L. Platt, P. Grenfell, P. G. Macioti. 2017. Reviewing the occupational risks of sex workers in comparison to other 'risky' professions. Available at: http://www2.le.ac.uk/departments/criminology/people/teela-sanders/teela-sanders.

Scott, J., V. Miichiello, R. Marino, G.P. Harvey, M. Jamieson, and J. Browne. 2005. Understanding the new context of the male sex work industry. *Journal of Interpersonal Violence* 20 (3): 320–342.

5

Policing Online Sex Markets

Abstract This chapter considers the legal and regulatory consequences of the increased use of digital technology in sex work. We consider how police are attempting to respond to a rapidly changing environment and the pressures this brings to traditional policing rationales and practices. The BtG study confirms that currently, there is limited awareness of online sex markets. In part, this is because policy and regulation in the UK has failed to pay attention to online markets and remains largely focused on street and managed indoor sectors. However, existing legislation may have significant consequences for the working conditions and security of people working in this sector. Laws relating to brothel keeping and initiatives that seek to tackle 'vulnerability' (to sexual exploitation or trafficking)—whilst clear policing priorities—may become the primary legal lenses through which *all* sex work is perceived. This creates significant challenges for policing online environments in terms of available resources and skills but also crucially in terms of balancing the rights and interests of the more diverse section/profile of industry that we describe in our study. We conclude by noting that these challenges are only exacerbated if policies and practices of policing do not better align with the realities of sex markets.

© The Author(s) 2018
T. Sanders et al., *Internet Sex Work*,
https://doi.org/10.1007/978-3-319-65630-4_5

Keywords Policing online markets · Regulation · Law reform
Prostitution policy · Modern slavery /trafficking · Data protection
Safety for sex workers

Introduction

While previous chapters have considered the Internet's impact on working practices in the sex industry, this section examines the legal and regulatory consequences as aspects of sex work increasingly move to an online environment. Our work and that of others shows evidence of an increased movement of sex workers into Internet-mediated private spaces (Cunningham and Kendall 2011; Peppet 2013), yet law enforcement has traditionally focused on more publicly visible forms of sex work. This, as Jones (2015) notes, begs the question: how are law enforcement agencies responding to these changes? At present, we know little beyond anecdote regarding the regulation and policing of digitally mediated forms of sex work. BtG is the first major research study to investigate how policing in the UK is endeavouring to deal with a rapidly changing market.

Informed by detailed interview data from participants involved in policing strategy and operations, managers of online platforms and from sex workers' own experiences, we look at how these fast-moving and hidden markets are a challenge to both the rationale and tactics of traditional policing. We look specifically at the state of current knowledge, the implications of this changing market for policing, and how information is gathered and analysed. Finally, we consider possible law reform, as we ask how can regulatory models better respond to the realities of commercial sex in the twenty-first century?

Legal and Policy Context

The legal and regulatory consequences of the increased use of digital technology in aspects of the sex industry are far from straightforward. Much depends on the legal position of sex work, the laws regarding advertising of sexual services, controls on obscene images and pornography and other ancillary legal controls that may apply to the use of digital technology. Laws vary across jurisdictions and there is considerable local variation in their implementation as a result of the interpretative nature of law, the use of discretion, the influence of various policing priorities and the relative attention given to sex work by law enforcement agencies.

In the USA, in the context of an almost blanket prohibition of prostitution, there are several ways in which online sex work may fall foul of the law (Larkin 2010). There has been targeted prosecution of sites for prostitution-related offences such as pimping and facilitating trafficking, including classified advertising websites hosting advertisements from sex workers and review sites (Peppet 2013). Indirect forms of online sex work such as webcamming may be also be proscribed, though there is some legal uncertainty as to whether this falls under laws relating to pornography or prostitution (Green 2002).

Moreover, the increased focus on anti-trafficking, which is high on the policy agenda in the USA and many European countries, frequently conceptualised in terms of sexual exploitation and targeted mainly by criminal justice responses, means the Internet has become a new site for police surveillance of sex work (Farrell and Cronin 2015; Jahnsen and Skilbrei 2017).

Regulation in the UK

Amidst a flurry of activities to control, shrink and displace street sex markets, online markets have continued to adapt and expand. Yet policy and legislation in the UK have failed to keep up with these developments and Internet-based sex markets exist within a vacuum of specific regulation (Ashford 2008). The Internet was mentioned only once in the *Paying the Price* consultation document (Home Office 2004, p. 21) and the regulatory responses under New Labour were based on protection for young people using the Internet (Barnardos 2004). In the All Party Parliamentary Group (2014) report on prostitution in the UK, the Internet was completely omitted. Rather incongruously, the Criminal Justice and Police Act 2001 (S46–47) law against telephone carding in public places was introduced despite high numbers of private online advertisements even at this time (Hubbard 2002). Currently, Internet controls and legislative changes in the UK have focused primarily upon pornographic images, for example, updating the Obscene Publications Acts of 1959 and 1964, with extreme pornography now rendered illegal under s63 of the Criminal Justice and Immigration Act 2008 (Carline 2011) and on ensuring age restrictions (e.g. The Digital Economy Act 2017).

Over more than a decade of intense prostitution policy and legal reform in the UK, the focus has primarily been on exploitation of women and the role of the purchaser of sexual services, which is often seen as intrinsically harmful. These narratives fail to reflect diversity in the sex industry, particularly within indoor markets (Sanders 2009; Pitcher 2015). Definitions of vulnerability in relation to commercial sex are still largely confined to areas such as exploitation of children and young people or, more recently, trafficking into the sex industry. Prostitution is frequently viewed as synonymous with human trafficking, with a great deal of legislative and police resources spent on combatting what is increasingly termed modern slavery (e.g. Modern Slavery Act 2015). Some jurisdictions, following Sweden's lead in criminalising purchasing sex, have introduced similar laws to target demand (e.g. Human Trafficking and Exploitation Act (Northern Ireland) 2015). Despite numerous attempts in Scotland, England and Wales to do the same, they have not, as yet, followed suit. Nevertheless, there is evidence of a 'creeping abolitionism' as purchasing sex is subject to increasing sanction and exiting is promoted (Scoular and Carline 2015).

One of the problems with a narrow political focus on sexual exploitation is that broader issues which affect sex workers, such as labour exploitation and rights, are neither recognised nor addressed. Although UK prostitution laws have tended to disregard market developments, existing legislation relating to issues such as brothel management and controlling for gain may impact negatively on the working conditions of independent sex workers, including those using the Internet (Pitcher 2015). While more recently in England and Wales the House of Commons Home Affairs Select Committee (2016) has acknowledged the changing composition and operation of the sex industry and has recommended amendments to the legislation to better protect sex workers, including those sharing premises, it is unclear whether these recommendations will be implemented.

These policy and regulatory trends raise a number of questions which we seek to address here. If there is a migration of sex workers into Internet-mediated private spaces, how are law enforcement agencies transforming their tactics and policies? Does the focus on trafficking and modern slavery mean that online advertisements are being monitored and surveilled and how do the police decide which laws to enforce and when?

Policing and Online Markets

Policy relating to policing of sex work has to date focused primarily on street sex work markets (Scoular and O'Neill 2007). Despite the decline of these markets (Matthews 2005) there has been very little focus on policing in indoor markets (Skilbrei 2001; Sanders 2009). In addition, both the laws in the UK and policing practices have frequently failed to acknowledge gender diversity in sex work, as well as new forms of virtual sexual exchange (Ashford 2008). We currently know little beyond anecdote as to how digitally mediated forms of sex work are policed (Jones 2015). The recent National Policing Sex Work Strategy for England and Wales (NPCC 2015) pays some attention to the changing context of sex work, taking the definition of online work from our BtG study,[1] and noting that its victim-centred approach (which seeks to balance public protection duties to sex workers with a proportionate response to community impacts) applies to all sectors of sex work.[2] Nonetheless, it is not clear to what extent this is being operationalised. In the sections that follow we draw on qualitative interviews with 56 representatives from police forces across the UK and 12 other participants managing online platforms or working with sex workers in some capacity, to explore the implications of market changes, intelligence gathering and current law enforcement operation processes in relation to online markets.

Awareness of Market Changes and Implications

This section considers perspectives of police representatives and others on market changes and the extent to which local policing practices have taken into account the implications of the move to Internet-based sex work. The majority of police interviewees acknowledged that sex markets had undergone significant changes in the last decade but knowledge of these new markets was variable. Many felt they were still learning about the nature and extent of Internet-based sex work in their force area and that intelligence about the sector was limited. Overall, the police response to online sex markets appeared undeveloped, although there were regional variations. This had been partly as a result of resourcing implications, but also because in some localities policing of sex markets has been reactive to complaints from residents or landlords and thus has frequently focused on the more visible aspects of sex work. Policy priorities and the National Policing Sex Work Strategy (NPCC 2015) also play a part and as discussed earlier, certain issues relating to concepts of risk and vulnerability, particularly around trafficking/modern slavery, have taken precedence over support for sex workers who do not fall into these categories. The interviews showed that for many police forces, the focus of operations locally has continued to be on street working and sometimes managed establishments such as massage parlours or saunas, although even these activities were spasmodic and often driven by complaints or alerts of potential criminal activities. Nonetheless, some interview participants were aware of changing markets and the need to develop more effective responses in relation to online sex work:

> …in effect the online issue has mainly arisen out of the National Guidance, because it's quite clear that there is a change going on… we have commissioned a profile in [this region] and I think it's fair to say it probably mirrors what's going on in the rest of the country in as much as the sort of historic picture of local girls working the street who have drug problems etc. is changing and I think what we're seeing is, much more now, girls are working, and men are working online, indoor sex work …although it's quite apparent that that is a real shift, I do feel as if the

police are sort of left behind to a degree, and we are still concentrating, probably for good reason, on the street work and...we have now those things in place in relation to National Ugly Mugs and everything to deal with that more effectively. But as this shift happens to the more online, indoor arena, I'm not entirely sure we're currently equipped to deal with that effectively. (Police interviewee)

Some participants, however, also observed that there will continue to be street and brothel work, partly because of the circumstances of some sex workers but also client preferences, for example, in terms of the relative costs of services. As one police interviewee observed: *'So although I personally think the internet will increase in size, I don't think we'll ever get rid of on-street'.*

There was some awareness amongst police officers that digital technologies have given sex workers new ways of contacting clients independently via their own websites or various advertising platforms. Some also observed that escort agencies and massage parlours have been advertising via the Internet:

And when we were speaking to the women and saying, "How are you finding the work," you know, I know they always say from a friend and, you know, they're not living in [this city] and they would quite often just say they would just put massage parlour, [this city], and invariably something would pop up. So [a general online classified advertising site] was one of them. There were a couple of other local sites that if you put in, it would come up and then they would look to make a phone call and get the work. (Police interviewee)

Nonetheless, others noted that it was more common to find sex workers who advertised online working independently on their own, or sometimes with another colleague: *'I think the vast majority are working alone ...there are couples advertising, male/female, female/female, but in the main it's—I would say it's females that are working independently'* (Police interviewee).

In the view of some police interviewees, online working was relatively safe compared with other markets, not only because there were fewer crimes against sex workers in this sector, but also because their exposure to enforcement activities was reduced. For example, one police officer commented: '*it's arguably a safer way of operating for all parties, in the sense of, it makes them... less exposed I suppose to enforcement activities, so you can only imagine that that will grow in time*'. There was also some perception that online working was less socially stigmatised than other forms of work such as street sex work. For instance, a police officer in another region observed that '*I wonder if it's [the increase in internet working] because it's also become a little bit more socially acceptable to become an escort......via the internet*'. Although online working might attract less police attention because of the reduced public visibility, some police interviewees also acknowledged that lone working might lead to increased vulnerability for some sex workers.

While, as discussed in Chap. 3, there is considerable diversity amongst sex workers in online markets, with some demographic differences compared with other sectors, sex work projects are also finding that some of their clients who previously worked on-street have moved to working via the Internet. Although this may reduce social stigma, as discussed earlier, it did not necessarily detract from the service needs experienced by those particular individuals:

> ...what we're seeing is where projects have been in place for many years and have been working with the same women, those women are now identifying themselves as private independent because they have a phone so they don't have to stand on the street, they can sit in their own homes and wait for those calls and they feel empowered to be classing themselves as private independent because there is that stigma around a street sex worker. So they're saying, 'No I'm a private independent' but the reality of [it is] that it's the same people with the same complex needs. (Service provider in safety scheme for sex workers)

There appeared to be little awareness amongst police interviewees of the significance of new forms of indirect cyber-exchange, such as webcamming. One police officer remarked that students appeared to be participating in webcam work, although, while concurring with the views earlier regarding relative safety, also perceived the potential for exploitation in some cases:

And apparently, a lot of them webcam. They webcam, but for convenience, and it is deemed to be slightly safer. Which I think, from a physical aspect, it is true, but they're still, still vulnerable, still at risk of different types exploitation, I think, with that. (Police interviewee)

Nonetheless, this participant did not specify what these types of exploitation might be. Although webcamming appears to be a relatively unobserved development by police forces in the UK, one online service provider commented that its increase coincides with a decline in traditional forms of commercial pornography. The growing popularity of more interactive platforms has also been noted by academic commentators and it has been suggested these new platforms differ from conventional mainstream pornography, particularly in giving performers greater control over the way in which they are represented. For example, Attwood (2013) discusses the development of alternative porn sites, which are frequently run by women. Nonetheless, as Figueira (2015, p. 132) notes: *'in adult live cams, the production of content relies on a balance between freely produced user-generated content and controls exerted by the market and the website company'*. Furthermore, Jones (2015) observes that webcam workers also face threats to their privacy through practices such as doxing, where information about sex workers' identity is acquired and shared, or capping, which involves copying and sharing of live performances without permission. Indeed our findings confirm this, as discussed further in Chap. 4. The interviews demonstrated that police forces currently have little knowledge of these new practices, yet there are legal and safety implications which have yet to be considered. There are thus potentially significant challenges for policing of online markets, as well as for developing support for sex workers who require it, which will be explored later in this chapter.

Implementation of current legislation and policies on Internet-based sex work

As some interview participants observed, more recent national guidance has changed the balance of policing priorities in relation to sex work generally. While the 2010 Prostitution Policy was seen as primarily concentrating on enforcement, in contrast, the current guidelines included in the National Policing Sex Work Strategy (2015): *'swings it completely the other way and we go for safeguarding now over enforcement'* (Police interviewee). Many police officers interviewed indicated they were happier with this approach. However, this also depended on the jurisdiction: for example, where the purchase of sexual services is criminalised, as in Northern Ireland, the suggestion was from some interviewees that this had increased sex workers' mistrust of the police. So there is sometimes an apparent tension between political moves to increase enforcement and the experience of police on the ground, who see this as contrasting with their role of 'keeping people safe', including sex workers. This distinction, however, may not be as apparent to those who are subject to 'help' when it is offered via the apparatus of criminal justice approach (Scoular and Carline 2015).

Nonetheless, although some police guidance may be moving towards greater protection of sex workers and consideration of their safety, the focus continues to be primarily in areas such as trafficking/modern slavery, child sexual exploitation or, in relation to online activities, implementing the Obscene Publications Acts discussed earlier. Governance of online advertising and display also comes under the purview of Ofcom, as well as the EU's Audiovisual Media Services Directive (AVMSD), which is currently under review. The scope of the AVMSD includes video-sharing platforms, but only in relation to either hate speech or dissemination of harmful content to minors.[3] However, as one legal expert participating in the BtG study observed, enforcement of legislation in this context *'is a Sisyphean task. It is utterly impossible to enforce in reality'*. Police interviewees also commented that enforcing laws relating to advertising of sexual services online may be problematic, because many host services are not based in the UK, so different jurisdictions apply. However, participants involved in web advertising noted that there was a degree of self-regulation amongst platforms:

> We certainly self-regulate as a business and we work with the relevant authorities. We don't, we make sure nothing illegal is happening. We try to provide links to support services. We're available to talk. We're not hidden. (Interviewee in leading adult platform)

As noted earlier, knowledge of online sex work amongst statutory authorities, both nationally and locally, is often partial and variable. Moreover, some police interviewees noted the difficulty in distinguishing between sex workers advertising online on their own behalf and people who might potentially be exploited, so unless suspicions are supported by intelligence from other sources '*you are guessing*'. There was a general feeling amongst research participants that the law is outdated and vague and, as one police participant observed '*things have moved on*'. A police officer in another region suggested that having flexibility to take a '*sensible and pragmatic approach*' may be helpful, although there are then possibilities that different forces will take different approaches if the legislation is unclear.

In many police force areas there was limited activity in relation to regulation of Internet-based sex work. As one police participant noted '*it's probably just monitoring it*', unless a specific crime was reported. A police interviewee in another region concurred with this approach, noting that similarly to other indoor markets: '*if they're not causing us a problem we don't want to be causing them a problem*'. So this included, for example, not taking covert initiatives to find out more about people advertising on online platforms. For some forces, therefore, the focus was on safety, but as the same participant commented, they need '*that backing from the government to acknowledge that safety's got to be the main priority*'. The lack of direction from government was noted:

> ... talking about the internet-enabled stuff, I mean in the real world we can't even regulate the stuff on the street, you know. There is no political will to challenge it or—to finally decide what we are going to do about sex workers. Are we going to help them, assist them live their lives and work? Are we going to criminalise them? Without that kind of politically, we can't do anything online. (Police interviewee)

It was suggested by some research participants, including online platforms for sexual services, some police officers and a legal expert in the field, that there needs to be further discussion regarding which aspects of sex work, including online pornography, are harmful or exploitative, rather than assuming that all forms of online sexual services are harmful per se. This also extends to the role of third parties seen to facilitate commercial sexual services. As discussed earlier, the way in which the law is currently enforced also impacts on Internet-based sex workers who work together. This was an issue raised not only by sex workers in the BtG study, but also police interviewees, some of whom noted that sex workers based collectively currently risk being penalised under existing legislation.

Safeguarding, vulnerability and trafficking discourses

Because national policy is linked to a focus on safeguarding, it does not include the potential for exploitation in voluntary sex work, so does not extend to labour protections, but only criminality in relation to issues such as slavery and child sexual exploitation. To an extent this was reflected in some of the interviews for the BtG study. For example, when discussing modern slavery/trafficking, some police participants distinguished between labour exploitation (which it appeared covers everything *outside* the sex industry) and sexual exploitation. In the small number of instances where exploitation of adult sex workers was raised, it was generally linked to the concept of control rather than other forms of exploitation in work.

The majority of police activities in relation to Internet platforms were within a modern slavery remit. There appeared generally to be less awareness of the independent/voluntary nature of much online sex work, except in a few instances where interview participants acknowledged that the issue of exploitation or slavery was less likely to arise in this context:

> … there's been no real reports of exploitation. The girls that would speak to me are – what I would say are generally single females who are just making a living and they've come across something that they haven't liked or behaviour towards them they haven't liked, but it's never been of exploitation or slavery or anything of that nature. (Police interviewee)

Another noted the difficulty in determining who might be trafficked/coerced and who might be working of their own volition, when considering migrant workers in the UK.

> We have—we might be able to recognise sex workers who we might know are advertising online, but how is that all facilitated from—from the start? Are they recruited? Do they know that they're coming in as sex workers? Because often they don't know. (Police interviewee)

However, to ascertain whether someone was sex working independently and/or of their own volition, or experiencing coercion, further investigation would be required: *'Whether it's of their own freewill, we'll only ever find out by interacting with that individual'* (Police interviewee). This is time-consuming, however, and requires adequate resourcing to follow up concerns effectively, as well as training for police officers visiting sex workers' premises, as some interview participants noted.

The interviews indicated there was sometimes uncertainty about the role of third parties: for example, were they merely facilitating the work of individuals, as indicated in Chap. 3, or was their involvement of a more coercive nature? As one police participant noted in relation to brothel management, there might be a possibility that *'the person running the premises is a victim but to make their own circumstances better for themselves, they've become almost slightly complicit within the network'*. Another police interviewee referred to a case where it was difficult to identify whether one man accompanying a migrant sex worker was there for the worker's own protection or whether he was a *'minder, as in curtailing the movements of the females and not letting them go out unaccompanied'*. This is made more complicated by migrant workers' distrust of the police and real fear of possible deportation, as discussed in Chap. 3, which may mean they are reluctant to divulge information. As several police interviewees noted, this made it difficult in their view to secure a prosecution.

The problem with a policing approach which assumes coercion and/or trafficking/slavery, however, is that unless handled sensitively, police activities will disrupt the business of those who are sex working legally of their own volition and may have the consequence of rendering online sex work more hidden, as discussed below. While enforcement and vulnerability issues were a key concern for some police interviewees, particularly those whose role related to trafficking/modern slavery, others also considered the safety of people who were sex working legally of their own volition. As one police participant noted: '*So for example, a sex worker that would work at home… they're situationally or circumstantially vulnerable because, you know, they're potentially allowing fifteen/twenty strange people in, into their home address a day*'. Some police interviewees were more aware of the need for a welfare-oriented, non-judgemental approach which would help to build trust among sex workers. This might include a more holistic approach which considered vulnerability more generally and engaged with sex workers as individuals, as well as organisations working with them:

> So in terms of what we focus on, we—of course we're focused on exploitation, trafficking, slavery, but we're focused on that within a much wider engagement strategy, not just around sex workers, but around victims of exploitation. (Police interviewee)

This broader approach was also seen to encourage reporting of other risks or crimes against sex workers. Nonetheless, there was frequently seen to be a tension between the enforcement and safeguarding agendas.

Police monitoring and activities relating to Internet-based sex work

Overall familiarity with online markets and intelligence gathering activities varied across the UK. In many instances police forces had not developed an organised approach to data collection and were aware their intelligence was limited. In part, as several police participants noted, this was because they did not have the up-to-date technology, dedicated funding or specialist staff resources to collect and interpret 'forensically sound' data. There is no national coordination of this monitoring, although during the period of interviewing, the National Police

Chiefs Council lead on sex work had requested a range of information from police forces in England and Wales. Despite limited resources, many police force areas who took part in the BtG study were considering, or had already commenced some form of scoping exercise into Internet-based sex work in their force area and some had already undertaken their own mapping exercise to inform their future approach. These varied in terms of the scope and methodology of the research. A common approach was where an officer/analyst had identified certain key online advertising platforms used by predominantly female sex workers and carried out counts for their area. Usually the platforms analysed were limited to a certain number, dependent on time and resources for the work. As policing of online markets was not a national priority, however, investigations into this area were often constrained to responses to complaints or concerns raised regarding safety or trafficking issues. One police participant observed:

> But it's not like we actively look, you know. We don't sit there with [a major online platform] and trawl through the site for [our city area] and get telephone numbers. We haven't got time to do that and it's not breaching the law anyway so it's not relevant for us until it becomes a problem for the community in terms of antisocial behaviour, and then we have to [be] a little bit more investigative.

Some police participants suggested it would be desirable to commission work with partners, which might in some cases include sex work projects, to gain a better understanding of online markets. Others recognised the rationale for a joined-up approach nationwide, because online work is not limited to geographical boundaries. However, cross-boundary cooperation again had implications for resourcing.

From the police interviews, a primary element of activities in relation to online sex markets was the identification of certain indicators of vulnerability and exploitation, which related to the policy priorities discussed earlier:

> We have a number of platforms ... where sex workers would advertise and our team, on a daily basis, would ... scan those websites looking for people

advertising … and looking for indicators that would help us ascertain or make an assessment that they're part of a broader network of organised prostitution and are likely not to be in control of their own destiny.

Factors such as sex worker mobility, payment mechanisms and types of sexual services offered were seen as potential signifiers of trafficking. Other indicators could be large numbers of visitors who only stay for a short time, consecutive mobile phone numbers in adverts, indicating that more than one SIM had been bought at the same time, different women in the same location, similarities between advertisements, or offering unprotected sex:

> …you can do it like geographic location, you can do it down to nationality, you can see their age, you can restrict their hair colour, you can do it by the sexual services they offer, and that's another key indicator really, anyone offering sort of unprotected sex is immediate alarm bells, because what person in their right mind would choose to do that. We've even been having profiles with women that are pregnant, clearly pregnant, advertising, there's a vulnerability risk there as well, so we've got to visit that. (Police interviewee)

As discussed in Chap. 3, there has been considerable recent media and policy attention to the apparent increase in 'pop-up brothels', with links frequently made to trafficking and exploitation. This narrative contrasts with the documented experience of independent sex workers, including migrant workers, who may travel to work in cities or tourist locations away from their home base for business purposes. Discussions on 'pop-up brothels' amongst police interviewees for the BtG study were often related to concepts of vulnerability and safeguarding, or the language of modern slavery/trafficking. Some forces identified activities on prominent online directories, investigating profiles of female sex workers which appeared spasmodically, in contrast with those which featured on a regular basis. The indicators of vulnerability discussed above were drawn on for these monitoring activities. Another focus of intelligence collection was consideration of whether the language used in advertisements indicated the sex workers were not native English speakers.

This was seen as a sign that the women concerned might be trafficked and they might then be visited by police to ascertain whether they were sex working of their own volition. Some police interviewees noted that where migrant workers were involved, the first assumption was they had been trafficked. Thus the onus appeared sometimes to be on the sex workers to prove that they were not trafficked or exploited, rather than their word being taken on trust, which could be difficult for them to achieve if their first language was not English.

Other police interview participants had greater awareness of voluntary sex work, however, and also commented on the restrictions in current policy and police strategy. For example, existing legislation does not allow for distinctions to be made between managed brothels and situations where two or more sex workers base themselves together for safety or convenience:

> And—but again, when you start looking at brothels, you have to think, right, well okay, well is it—is it just a couple of sex workers who've got themselves together and they—they're running a brothel, or are they all working for somebody else, in which case that would fall back under the slavery act. (Police interviewee)

Police visiting premises had to use their judgement when speaking to individual sex workers, to determine whether to refer them to a specialist officer such as a Sexual Offences Liaison Officer (SOLO). There was some consciousness that certain indicators used might also flag up sex workers who were not trafficked or otherwise exploited, although this was not the intention of specialist teams:

> …we're not targeting sex work, you know. We've got miles better priorities than targeting—we're not a team that targets sex work. So we're only targeting exploitation and vulnerability in sex work, yeah. (Police interviewee)

The potential implications of such police actions are disruption of sex workers' business, stigmatisation and potential threats to their safety if they are forced to change working practices or move from their current premises because their privacy has been compromised.

Implications for sex workers' safety

The section above highlights a potential conflict between police monitoring activities within a modern slavery agenda and sex workers' civil liberties. As discussed in Chap. 4, sex workers are keen to take their own safety measures to protect their identity online, which may be undermined by police surveillance and enforcement. A concern expressed by some police interviewees was that their online activities might lead sex workers to move their advertising, which has been the experience in the Republic of Ireland and the USA (Finn and Stalans 2016).

> So I think, from what I'm gathering through [a major platform] and stuff like that, is it's something that we can go on and look without causing any issue. And what we don't wanna do is for them to go to secret sites that we don't know about, because that's generally where the nasty people will go and look so they can't be traced. (Police interviewee)

Certain interview participants, such as representatives of sex worker-led safety schemes, expressed concern that local police forces seemed to have little awareness of the safety concerns and support needs of sex workers advertising online, which impacted on their ability to deal with crimes against them. The survey of sex workers also showed that relatively few Internet-based sex workers had experienced direct contact with the police during their work, but of those who had, only 2.8% ($n = 18$) had been provided with information on safety in sex work by the police. While, as discussed in Chap. 3, sex workers may sometimes feel more secure as a result of lack of police attention to their activities, particularly because enforcement operations are detrimental to their safety and working conditions, as Pitcher and Wijers (2014) have observed, many sex workers would welcome greater support and workplace protection from the police. A police interview participant in the

BtG study acknowledged the need to engage further with sex workers in online markets, to address safety concerns:

> ... it is a concern [i.e. shift to individual working] ...because I think the more hidden it becomes the more difficult it is for us to engage, for us to understand the ... vulnerabilities... we need to understand the threat posed by, why people who are potentially being drawn towards that area of business as a client really. And it's... difficult because we don't understand the extent of that, but there will be, I have no doubt, you know sex offenders who we know about, or alternatively who we don't know about who perhaps we should know about who will engage in that marketplace ... because we're not as closely, I don't think, as engaged with the workers as we perhaps could be. And then if you take that market ... online, as opposed to on-street, then it becomes even more clandestine and more difficult to engage with. (Police interviewee)

While a small number of police participants were more aware of the types of online crimes perpetrated against sex workers, such as harassment/stalking, threats or using personal information gathered online, currently this appeared to be a minority of forces interviewed. Although there is legislation to address some of these crimes, forces have not necessarily been proactive in informing sex workers and it was recognised further work needs to be undertaken in this area:

> As part of the wider regulatory framework police forces need to communicate clearly that such activity is criminal, encourage sex workers to report such crimes and be prepared to investigate such crimes with sensitivity and ensure sex workers who are victims of such crime are supported. (Police interviewee)

Some police participants suggested it would be useful to have a link on major platforms to offer support and safety messages:

> What I would like to see is ... in an ideal world ... some sort of link on [Platform 1] site or [Platform 2] or whatever it was that said, 'This is your police link and we're here to help, you know, if you need something' so that we could reach out to more people. (Police interviewee)

There was also some acknowledgement that police officers may need educating on the legal situation in order to be responsive to sex workers and to balance that against unnecessary intrusion into their lives. Without a consistent national policy, however, it was recognised that local police strategies might alter as personnel changed. Moreover, the interviews with many police officers, with certain exceptions, indicated a broad lack of awareness of Internet-based sex workers' own safety information and advice networks, some of which already operated via major online platforms, sex worker-led websites or national schemes such as National Ugly Mugs. While there was some recognition that there were sex worker-led schemes and preparedness to work with these, this knowledge did not appear to be widespread amongst police participants.

Police interaction with online advertising platforms

Many police forces interviewed had limited interaction with online companies, particularly as some are not UK-based which may complicate communication. While some police interviewees were familiar with and used specific links on major international platforms for criminal justice-related enquiries or reporting, it appeared others were not aware of this facility. Some forces used certain major platforms to search for information, but many did not engage directly with the managers of these platforms, except occasionally in relation to specific operations. There were mixed reports on the response, with some participants finding varied cooperation. For example, one police interviewee commented on the experience of colleagues when running an operation: *'they contacted some of these companies and they said some were really helpful, others were, "'[I]t's got nothing to do with you".'* However, another reported a more positive experience:

> I found [a major online platform] very helpful…They came back in a really timely manner with the information that we needed, that…we are able to progress because it was a safeguarding issue, the one that I'm thinking of, involving young people—yeah, no issues at all, found them very helpful. (Police interviewee)

In some instances police would go through an intermediary, such as National Ugly Mugs or an online escort forum, to facilitate interaction. It was noted justification was needed for information requests, particularly because of data protection regulations and protocols. This was helpful for building relations, as companies might be suspicious of approaches from the police, because of the recent operations targeting online platforms in the USA, and also because some platforms had themselves experienced enforcement activities:

> ... as with any partnership, if you engage appropriately and show a measured proportion of response and that your requests are targeted against criminality ... you will get assistance more willingly than if you are recklessly ... targeting willing sex workers, you know, without any discernment. Then, because that is ultimately the platforms, that is their business and that is not an unlawful business, so we rely on that cooperation. (Police interviewee)

This was also noted by an interviewee in a UK-wide online advertising platform, who stated they would cooperate with police requests: '*if it's a reasonable request, it sounds legal and proper, yeah*'. Online companies interviewed emphasised that where there were legitimate concerns about criminal activities, including human trafficking, child exploitation or coercion of adults, they were diligent in helping with enquiries: '*it's a perfectly legal business, we operate within the law and ... our relationships with the police are very important*'. One police participant suggested it would be helpful if companies were more proactive and contacted the police if they had concerns about specific profile users, but it was also recognised there were data protection concerns and the companies had their own business priorities. Companies also operated according to the relevant data protection/sharing laws in their host country, and thus police forces may have to comply not only with UK laws, but also legal requirements in other countries.

> ...we need to make sure that whatever we do adheres to PIPA, which is the Personal Information Protection Act and it is a Canadian law, which is very strict in terms of when and how we can release any kind of personal information. So, we work with the police if they need any kind of

> information, but they need to follow those PIPA-related regulations...So just somebody calling in, that I'm from this police etc., I need this information, we're not going to release it. They need to do the proper legal process and then if we get that...we do provide them with the information but...they need to have ... like a judge needs to validate it, so... it's a really strict process. (Participant, international online dating and advertising site)

There was thus understandable caution on the part of online platforms when engaging with police forces to ensure their actions complied with the appropriate legislation and also protected the interests and online security of customers who were acting within the law. There was also some feeling on the part of certain police participants that greater cooperation should be encouraged, which means a different approach on their part, moving away from an enforcement focus to work more collaboratively:

> ... if they can provide us information and if they can work with us and they can help us with intelligence and helping and safeguarding people who are vulnerable, then...we need to look at the fact that people genuinely use that service in order to advertise because they want to do that line of work and what they are doing is not illegal in, in certain circumstances. So you know removing [a major platform] would only cause the issue to go somewhere else, you can't combat the issue by enforcement, and it'd be silly to think you can. So, you know, you need to be able to work with an organisation in order to try and legislate, in order to try and stop...the serious forms of criminality and ensure that we've got a way of identifying that. (Police interviewee)

It was also recognised this was a longer-term consideration, particularly as it would involve extensive relationship building, given the often fragile nature of relations between the police and third parties in the sex industry.

Data protection legislation and implications

As discussed above, there were clear data protection concerns regarding exchange of information between police forces and online advertising platforms. In addition, data protection laws governed information sharing with other agencies and also surveillance activities, which affected monitoring of online communications. While police were able to access open source materials, certain legislation, such as the Regulation of Investigatory Powers Act 2000 (RIPA) and its Scottish equivalent (RIPSA), determined which monitoring activities were feasible:

> Yes, we're restricted by RIPA and RIPSA which is the regulation of surveillance basically, so all about doing surveillance and we generally can't willy-nilly keep going onto the sites, the same sites, the same Facebook pages and things like that. We have to have an authority to do it, to start looking at it. So we're restricted by that, and it's maybe going to be more targeted for a particular problem, then we could justify looking at these sort of sites. (Police interviewee)

There were also data protection implications for recording and sharing information within police forces. For instance, information on Ugly Mugs reports has to be worded in a particular way when recording alleged offences on computer systems, to protect the identity of sources. There are also clearance levels within police forces for access to certain data.

Some police interviewees noted data protection concerns expressed by sex workers reporting crimes, particularly that their information would not be shared with other departments. For example, one interviewee had encountered concerns that sharing information with personnel with a human trafficking brief might lead to risks of deportation. Online advertising platforms also had considerations regarding protection of sex workers' identity under the UK Data Protection Act. Concerns included the possibility of being hacked or mishandling of data, allowing it to enter the public domain. As discussed above, justification needed to be provided by police forces before disclosure of personal information and one participant in a leading international platform noted that if there was any doubt about someone's eligibility to be provided with data then a court order would be required to disclose information about individual members. Another interviewee from a UK-wide platform stated that, as a safeguard, '*Nothing goes on our website without going through human moderation*'. Another platform noted the importance of keeping any personal data on an encrypted drive to prevent hacking.

While it was acknowledged that greater information sharing might be beneficial for pursuing crimes such as human trafficking, as well as crimes against sex workers, in some instances limited knowledge of data protection legislation and concerns presented an obstacle to cooperation between agencies:

> Misunderstanding of data protection issues is probably the single most important barrier to effective multi-agency working. Provided information is shared properly in order to further a policing need in a way that is proportionate, lawful and necessary, there need not be unnecessary concerns. The Children's Act provides further protection in this regard in relevant cases and Information Sharing Agreements outlining how information should be managed can alleviate concerns raised by partner agencies. (Police interviewee)

Views on Law Reform

There were diverse views amongst participants from all groups consulted on how sex work should be regulated. In part, this related to the complexities of the current legislation, as well as lack of knowledge of the different options that might be feasible. Thus, this section is indicative only and should not be taken as comprising tangible suggestions for law reform.

The survey of sex workers ($n = 641$) indicated that the majority of respondents felt offering or advertising indirect or direct sexual services online and purchasing these services should be legal, as should working in the same premises with other sex workers and the involvement of third parties such as online platforms, receptionists or landlords in facilitating sexual services. While there were mixed opinions as to how regulation should apply (i.e. whether sex work and associated activities should be regulated in the same way as any other form of work, or whether there should be specific licensing applied), qualitative responses to the survey indicated many respondents had insufficient knowledge of the implications of different legal approaches to make that judgement. The main emphases in the text comments were on rights, labour protection and support for sex workers. Very few respondents felt that direct or indirect sex work should be illegal: no more than 2–3% of respondents in most instances, although 8% of respondents ($n = 54$) felt involvement of managers, receptionists or landlords in facilitating sexual services should be illegal. Text responses to the survey indicated that some people holding this view had experiences of exploitation in managed premises in the past, or had concerns about the high premiums charged by some third parties. However, the text responses from respondents stating that involvement of third parties should be legal suggested any future legislation should address exploitative workplace practices and give greater protection to sex workers. For instance, a female independent escort/webcammer in her late twenties stated that what she wanted was:

> Full decriminalisation of sex work, the introduction of full labour rights, and a concerted effort to break down the stigma that affects us. I want to be able to work with my friends for safety without fearing arrest.

As some survey respondents observed, decriminalisation would still mean criminal activities such as slavery/trafficking or coercive practices could be tackled, as these are covered under different laws, as with other industries. However, as one female webcam worker in her late thirties observed, work through digital platforms may be viewed as similar to other 'gig' economy jobs in terms of questionable management practices and working conditions such as low wages, and '*not all jobs that are considered self-employment are true opportunities for entrepreneurship*'. To change the regulatory framework for sex work, therefore, would not necessarily end exploitative practices, but this is an issue to be addressed that extends beyond the sex industry.

Police interview participants also acknowledged inconsistencies in the interpretation of current laws relating to sex work and to online activities in particular. Some were sympathetic to arguments for decriminalisation, although as discussed above, there would still need to be regulation of some kind to address potential exploitation in managed premises. There were diverse views as to what form this regulation would take, with some interviewees aware that there was the potential for creating a dual labour market. This has been noted in relation to other jurisdictions, such as in the Netherlands (Pitcher and Wijers 2014):

> ...if you do get a regulating body, what's going to happen then is you'll have your prostitutes and people buying sex in the legal framework and then you'll have your brothels, the underground brothels...where you have got the exploited because they're not regulated. (Police interviewee)

Where further criminalisation had been introduced, as in Northern Ireland, where the purchase of sexual services is now a criminal offence, this was seen to have created difficulties in implementation for the police, particularly because of the mistrust discussed earlier. This could lead to fewer reports of criminal activities or abusive behaviour:

> Because if you're dealing with somebody who's complaining about a particular person's behaviour towards them they're reluctant to report it because ... they think police might want to report that person for paying for sex, and that doesn't encourage people to report things or speak to police. ... I mean, when that law actually came through I noticed a big decrease in anybody contacting me. (Police interviewee)

There were mixed opinions regarding the regulation of advertising and providing sexual services online. A small number of police interviewees felt there should be more stringent regulation of websites promoting sexual services, although others raised problems with this approach. One concern in relation to Internet-based sex work, as touched upon earlier, was that existing cooperation between sex workers, police and websites could be reduced through greater regulation:

> There's a danger of the more you legislate the more underground you drive it because, at the moment, traffickers will utilise these web services, these websites, and if we can get to that information to safeguard people, then that's great. If we can create more legislation to naturally safeguard people without driving it underground, then that would be good, yes. But I think my fear would certainly be that if you legislate, then they will go onto less legitimate websites. (Police interviewee)

Web companies interviewed also noted the problems of further regulation of online advertising, which did not take into account rapidly changing technology and, rather than preventing or addressing criminal practices such as trafficking would lead to *'more secrecy and… more danger to both parties'* (Moderator of online platform). People who wanted to could find a way around enforcement and it would be detrimental to legitimate consensual interactions between sex workers and clients. While, as discussed above, there is a degree of self-regulation on the part of online platforms, some police participants felt these platforms could do more to monitor the placing of advertisements to ascertain whether coercion might be involved. However, some police participants and also web companies also suggested it would be more effective to improve mechanisms for sex workers to report crimes to the police or via third parties. This might be within a framework of more general decriminalisation or legalisation of sex work, which would provide an environment where sex workers might feel more supported in making reports.

While there were not consistent views on mechanisms for regulating sex work, however, a general consensus amongst all research participants was that the priority was to ensure greater safety and protection for sex workers. This might at the very minimum involve allowing a small number of direct or indirect sex workers to share premises without fear of prosecution. To be effective, this would need to be nationwide, which again raised the need for a more strategic approach to sex work generally:

> ...because we're saying there's two and three people in a, a premises so we're comfortable with that because we know you're safer. But it would be much better for everybody if legislation reflected that to whatever number, you know, whether it's three or four, wherever they sit comfortably... (Police interviewee)

Conclusions

The BtG study confirms that currently there is limited awareness of online sex markets and the implications for policing, which largely remains focused on street and managed indoor sectors. In part, this is because policy and regulation in the UK have failed to pay attention to online markets, not only in relation to direct sex workers advertising online, but also newer forms of indirect online-only commercial sexual exchanges. Nonetheless, although the Internet-based sex industry is rarely acknowledged in UK policy and law, existing legislation may have significant consequences for the working conditions and security of people working in this sector.

While there has been a more recent move from enforcement to safeguarding in recent national police guidance, policy documents frequently draw on particular conceptions of 'vulnerability', related primarily to sexual exploitation of young people, women and victims of trafficking when discussing the sex industry. UK policies and regulatory instruments do not take into account the diversity of online markets, or problems relating to the human rights or safety of independent sex workers or those in other sectors who are working of their own volition. This also includes migrant workers, who appear to be targeted in specific operations, for example, against 'pop-up brothels'. Moreover, diversity amongst third parties is not generally understood and their roles are typically associated with exploitation and other forms of control.

Police monitoring of online activities appears variable and often spasmodic. Similarly, there is relatively limited interaction with online advertising platforms. In some cases relations were positive, but it appears police do not always understand the data protection and other legal protocols which govern platforms' ability to share data and their need to protect the identity of customers working within the law. There was some recognition that more punitive policing approaches may drive online sex work and networks further underground, making it harder to reach individuals and also to address crimes against them. Nevertheless, the inconsistencies in current policy and variable approaches to enforcement across regions, as well as experiences of intrusive policing practices in other jurisdictions, led to continued mistrust of the police amongst sex workers and online platforms. This could also impact on the extent to which sex workers reported crimes to the police, as discussed earlier in this book. It was that there needs to be greater clarity and political leadership on priorities and how to balance safeguarding of sex workers, including adults working of their own volition, with enforcement of laws relating to criminal activities in the sector.

While there was no clear consensus on the appropriate regulatory framework for online sex markets, there was general agreement that sex workers' safety and protection should be paramount. There were also indications from some of the interviews with police and other research participants, as well the survey of sex workers, that criminalisation, including of clients, is detrimental to sex workers' safety. The findings in this chapter point to the need for a more strategic approach to sex work which does not penalise sex workers or involve activities which make it a more hidden and hard-to-reach industry.

Notes

1. As described in the Introduction of the book we define internet-based sex work as '*Sex workers based on their own, or in collectives, or working through an agency, who use the internet to market or sell sexual services either directly (i.e. Interacting with clients in person e.g. Escorting, erotic massage, BDSM*) or indirectly (i.e. interacting with clients online e.g. web camming).'
2. Police Scotland's Prostitution Policy 2016 (http://www.scotland.police.uk/assets/pdf/151934/151938/prostitution-policy?view=Standard) follows a similar brief but does not mention this sector.
3. https://ec.europa.eu/digital-single-market/en/revision-audiovisual-media-services-directive-avmsd, accessed 4th July 2017.

References

All Party Parliamentary Group. 2014. *Shifting the burden: Prostitution and the global sex trade*. London: HMSO.

Ashford, C. 2008. Sex work in cyberspace: Who pays the price? *Information and Communications Technology Law* 17 (1): 37–49.

Attwood, F. 2013. Through the looking glass? Sexual agency and subjectification online. In *New femininities: postfeminism, neoliberalism and subjectivity*, ed. R. Gill and C. Scharff. Basingstoke: Palgrave Macmillan.

Barnardos. 2004. *Just one click: Sexual abuse of children and young people through the internet and mobile phone technology*. Ilford: Barnardos.

Carline, A., and Scoular, J. 2017. Almost abolitionism: The peculiarities of prostitution policy in England and Wales. In E. Ward and G. Wylie, *Feminism, prostitution and the state: The politics of neo-abolitionism*. Abingdon: Routledge.

Carline, A. 2011. Criminal justice, extreme pornography and prostitution: Protecting women or promoting morality? *Sexualities* 14 (3): 312–333.

Cunningham, S., and T.D. Kendall. 2011. Prostitution 2.0: The changing face of sex work. *Journal of Urban Economics* 69 (3): 273–287.

Farrell, A., and S. Cronin. 2015. Policing prostitution in an era of human trafficking enforcement. *Crime Law and Social Change* 64 (4–5): 211–228.

Figueira, J. M. 2015. *Global affective network: An analysis of paid adult live cams*. PhD thesis, University of Melbourne. http://hdl.handle.net/11343/127924.

Finn, M., and L. Stalans. 2016. How targeted enforcement shapes marketing decisions of pimps: Evidence of displacement and innovation. *Victims and Offenders* 11 (4): 578–599.

Green, M. 2002. Sex on the internet: a legal click or an illicit trick. *California Western Law Review* 38 (2), Article 9.

Home Office. 2004. *Paying the Price: A Consultation on Prostitution*. London: Home Office.

House of Commons Home Affairs Committee. 2016. *Prostitution: Third report of session 2016–17. HC 26*. London: House of Commons. http://www.publications.parliament.uk/pa/cm201617/cmselect/cmhaff/26/26.pdf.

Hubbard, P. 2002. Maintaining family values? Cleansing the streets of sex advertising. *Area* 34 (4): 353–360.

Jahnsen, S., and M.-L. Skilbrei. 2017. Leaving no stone unturned: The borders and orders of transnational prostitution. *British Journal of Criminology*. doi:10.1093/bjc/azx028.

Jones, A. 2015. Sex work in a digital era. *Sociology Compass* 9 (7): 558–570.

Larkin, J.E. 2010. Criminal and civil liability for user generated content: Craigslist, a case study. *Journal of Technology Law and Policy* 15: 85.

Matthews, R. 2005. Policing prostitution ten years on. *British Journal of Criminology* 45 (6): 877–895.

National Police Chiefs' Council (NPCC). 2015. *National Policing Sex Work Strategy*. http://library.college.police.uk/docs/NPCC/National-Policing-Sex-Work. Accessed 10 July 2017.

Peppet, S.R. 2013. Prostitution 3.0? *Iowa Law Review* 98: 1989–2060.

Pitcher, J. 2015. Sex work and modes of self-employment in the informal economy: Diverse business practices and constraints to effective working. *Social Policy and Society* 14 (1): 113–123. doi:10.1017/S1474746414000426.

Pitcher, J., and M. Wijers. 2014. The impact of different regulatory models on the labour conditions, safety and welfare of indoor-based sex workers. *Criminology and Criminal Justice* 14 (5): 549–564.

Sanders, T. 2009. UK sex work policy: Eyes wide shut to voluntary and indoor sex work. In *Regulating sex for sale: Prostitution policy reform in the UK*, ed. J. Phoenix. Bristol: Policy Press.

Scoular, J., and A. Carline. 2015. A critical account of a 'creeping neo-abolitionism': Regulating prostitution in England and Wales. *Criminology and Criminal Justice* 14 (5): 608–626.

Scoular, J., and M. O'Neill. 2007. Regulating Prostitution: Social inclusion, responsibilization and the politics of politics of prostitution reform. *British Journal of Criminology* 47 (5): 764–778.

Skilbrei, M.-L. 2001. The rise and fall of the Norwegian massage parlours: Changes in the Norwegian prostitution setting in the 1990s. *Feminist Review* 67 (1): 63–77.

6

Conclusion: Key Messages

Abstract The conclusion draws out some key messages from Beyond the Gaze which has assessed the impact of digital technologies on work, safety, crimes and policing. Technology has indelibly shaped contemporary forms of commercial sex, but quantifying this market is difficult. Online mediums provide greater fluidity, flexibility and autonomy, but there are also disadvantages, unpredictable earnings, privacy issues and enduring stigma. The interaction between digital technologies and sex work is producing new forms of labour and variations in the processes of commercial sex, some of which are adapted versions of pre-Internet sex work, others entirely new, such as webcamming. BtG found online and digital technologies play an important role within Internet-based sex worker's safety practices. Online facilitation methods, such as screening through digital tools feature in many worker's safety repertoires, often combined with non-digital 'old school' methods which pre date the online sex work revolution. Yet technology has a dual-edged impact and can be used to facilitate crimes against sex workers, generating new harms and risk's of privacy violations. BtG confirms that currently, there is limited awareness of online sex markets, partly because UK policy and regulation has failed to pay attention to online markets and remains largely focused on street and managed indoor sectors. However, existing legislation and policy around brothel keeping and modern slavery may have significant consequences for working conditions and security of people working in this sector. The Internet has become an important means of connecting sex workers, enabling information sharing, mutual support and activism.

Keywords Mapping · Flexibility in sex work · Labour processes Digital risks · Blended safety strategies · Peer support · Activism Online sex worker spaces

The Online Market: It's Big but Difficult to Quantify

From our extensive observations and knowledge of the online sex industries and assessing how sex workers, platform managers and website owners categorise their businesses and activities, we have developed a sense of how the online 'sexscapes' operate (Brennan 2004), what they look like and their functions. Digital technologies have significantly shaped contemporary forms of sexual commerce. New forms of marketing strategies, business models, professional networking and activism have arisen in the last decade and become key game changers. We note that the advertising platforms for sexual services are extensive, providing larger commercial platforms for sex worker escort profiles which operate as the 'go to' online spaces for sex workers and customers alike, as well as more niche (by sexual service/preference or gender specific service) platforms, providing specific spaces for interested parties. Some of these different forms of platforms, including escort directories, can also be categorised as multi functional because they facilitate webcamming and/or instant messaging/SMS chat. In addition, some platforms are used solely for webcam performances. Customer review forums, mainly relating to female online sex work, are part of the terrain. Commercial sex businesses in the UK (such as agencies or brothels) often run their own websites, profiling the workers and taking inquiries. These are all in addition to individual sex worker websites, where workers will host their own website, control their content and online interactions with customers.

6 Conclusion: Key Messages

Commercial sex can also be traceable in classified advertising websites (the ones that sell anything such as Gumtree, Craigslist) as well as across social media platforms. More recently, dating/hook-up sites, including those also used for commercial advertising, have been frequented by those selling and buying sex, although invariably such platforms have strict non-commercial policies. Closed or member only spaces have been identified for sex workers only, where forums operate as a professional business network as well as a space for sharing resources, advice and activism. Content delivery platforms are dedicated platforms that host and sell user-generated adult content online. This is usually where the sex worker creates their own content and the site provides the necessary technology and financial services for clients to purchase this content. The platform takes a percentage of any sale, and the sex worker has the control over the content, who sees it and how much they charge. These commercial relationships between sex workers and websites with specific technological features are increasingly the norm as sex workers pay third parties for online space, storage and tech expertise.

With so many different spaces where commercial sex happens, the expansiveness and presence of the online sex markets are huge. Yet at the same time, there are difficulties in trying to get a handle on the online commercial sex market, to calculate the extent of the online commercial sex and numbers of people involved. We have confirmed that attempts to quantify the number of sex workers are highly problematic even when data are provided from original sources of advertising platforms. As explained in detail in Chap. 2, our own counts of sex worker profiles on the main advertising site for UK escorts show that the front-facing profiles (the individual profiles that browsers actually see) are not an accurate account of how many active sex workers are operating. We compared our front facing counts of profiles collected three times a year from May 2016 to June 2017 with that from the main platforms own data of registered active profiles. There were sometimes as much as forty per cent discrepancy in the front-facing data compared to the platforms own data on active profiles. The challenges of quantifying the online sex industry by counting profiles are evident as the problem of multiple and inactive profiles distorts any estimate, making the any estimate/the process problematic. Attempts to quantify by police forces, support or campaign organisations and the media should be approached within this context and the limitations to mapping based on front-facing profile data acknowledged.

Fluidity and Flexibility in Work

The nature of sex work that is facilitated through online methods, or supplied directly online, is changing because of the advantages presented/offered by utilising online mediums. Most respondents ($n = 615$) worked in what can be categorised as independent indoor sectors, that is: independent sex workers/escorts, webcam workers, providers of sexual massage or BDSM services. Whilst the profile of the survey respondents suggests more people who do not have dependents are engaged in sex work, there were some differences in age between those only doing webcam and those taking on both escorting and webcam work. Younger people tended to be more active in the Web-based services offering Web modelling and phone sex. Most people were working in more than one sector, but 42% ($n = 267$) were just escorting. The isolated nature of the work is striking, given that 72% ($n = 462$) worked alone.

What we know about the demographics of work patterns also helps explain the increasingly fluid nature of sex work. Sex work is often not always the primary mode of work and is often undertaken on a part time or sporadic basis, with sex workers using the features of digital technology, particularly advertising to manage their time and labour. In our interviews, 34 participants worked in other labour sectors ranging from health and social care ($n = 5$) to administration/clerical ($n = 4$), some working in more than one, and 6 were students. Flexibility is key: some sex workers are highly mobile, moving geographically (touring) to provide services in different parts of the country (occasionally country hopping), or working for bursts of time rather than on a regular basis. The simple features of advertising profiles enable this fluid interaction with the customer base, giving individuals more choice over when and where they work. Given very few pay a third party to assist them in any aspect of their work (other than advertising platforms who are paid to market profiles), the levels of control over their businesses were high. Working conditions were largely considered to be enhanced due to the possibilities offered by digital technologies. Chapter 3 explores how respondents described improved quality over their working life, control over their working conditions and increased ability to develop and build their own businesses online. Disadvantages centred around the increased number of hours spent managing their business online being one of the main disadvantages of online sex work ranked alongside stigma and privacy issues. Whilst some of these disadvantages were somewhat offset by the relative autonomy over working patterns, there were challenges to report. Problems noted significantly in Chap. 4 are the digital risks that have become inherent in working online in a sector, where there are threats to privacy through crimes such as doxing and the misuse of information.

Labour Processes Through Digital Technologies

The discussions on the types of labour processes that sex workers engage in are now relatively extensive (see Wolkowitz et al. 2013; Pitcher 2014). Emotional labour strategies (Brewis and Linstead 2000; Brents et al. 2010), psychological strategies (Sanders 2001, 2005), as well as the physicality of doing sex work provide rich detailed understandings of the complexities of selling sex as many different forms of labour and not simply just sexual (Smith 2017). The interaction between digital technologies and sex work is producing new forms of labour and variations in the processes of commercial sex, some of which are refined and adapted versions of what we already know about doing sex work, but others are entirely new, made possible by the existence of online sex markets such as webcamming. Some of the labour processes around the management of the identity and the presentation of the self are simply enhanced because of the online terrain: controlling images, switching profile photos; enticing customers by refreshing pages with new images and description is now all part of the everyday management of the online identity. For many, use of social media regarding their work profiles was another aspect of both identity and business management.

Jones (2015: 561) notes that the Internet has created new spaces for commercial sexual services and goods and has made a difference to sex workers' working practices and conditions—not only enhancing safety procedures, but also enabling people to work across different sectors, such as escorting and webcam performances, as well as potentially improving wages. For those sex workers who move across both the webcam and escorting markets, expertise in several types of labour processes is needed to fulfil each role. Emotional labour has been well established as a core labour process of all types of sex work activities including webcamming where social interaction, conversation, listening and caring characteristics are needed. The labour needed to present the self (in whatever sex-guise required) is complex as both in-person and digital only services can emphasize body scrutiny, performance and interaction. However, as noted further in the conclusion, the creation of 'intimacy' is important whether working digitally or in-person. The skills, emotional intelligence, and the reading of the customer to make money through the webcam are possibly more intense than the off line in-person interaction where there is usually more prelude, more time and obviously more physical 'real time' interaction.

The opportunities provided by digital technologies for sex workers mean that money can be made from their bodies in abstentia. So, for example, selling content (sexualised images of their body or sex videos) is becoming an increasing part of online sex workers repertoires as this makes cash with very little physical input other than the initial performance. Also, sex workers sell access to their various online accounts (such as Instagram), making money out of posting non-sexualised images about their everyday lives no different to the new work form of 'vlogging', where individuals make content in video form to add to their space in the blogosphere. For sex workers, the updating and maintaining of profiles (or other media) have begun to take the traditional element of labour processes identified in the literature as part of sex work into new realms. In post modern sex work information technology, labour processes demand that organisational business skills are as equally important as body presentation and image. Beyond the Gaze has confirmed that the diversity of labour processes in sex work is increasing and workers are often switching rapidly, between labour types.

Online Crimes, Digital Risks and 'Blended' Safety Strategies

Beyond the Gaze has found that online and digital technologies play an important role within Internet-based sex worker's safety practices. Online facilitated methods, such as screening through digital tools feature in many worker's safety repertoires, often combined with non-digital 'old school' methods most of which pre date the online sex work revolution. Online and digital technology has provided new opportunities for sex workers to improve screening and wider safety routines, indeed in the growing body of international research about Internet mediated sex work the ability of technology to improve screening and safety is a salient theme (Ashford 2009; Cunningham and Kendall 2011; Peppet 2013; Ray 2007). Our research (Chap. 4) shows how online platforms, applications and smart phone technology have been keenly used by online sex workers in the UK as a core part of the safety strategies they employ. Embracing such technologies for safety is also one of the ways online sex workers have utilised and developed their digital skills. Chapter 4 provides an overview of the importance of online technology for safety and describes how online strategies are now blended with offline safety measures.

However, there is also the potential for the technology to facilitate crimes against sex workers, generating new harms and presenting greater risk of exposure and privacy violations. Building on the initial findings from Sanders et al. (2016), the 'new' crimes which are digitally facilitated (such as doxing or the misuse of information) add new occupational risks to what we know about violence against sex workers. Whilst reports of sexual assault, physical assault or threat of violence were relatively small as reported in the last five years, the average number of different types of crime experienced in the past 12 months was three. As detailed in Chap. 4, the everyday nature of victimisation was through digitally mediated crimes, particularly abusive, persistent and unwanted texts, emails and contact through social media. In coming years when police data on digital crimes/victimisation is readily available in annual reporting, it will be key to compare what we have found out in relation to sex workers with the general population to beable to comment on the broader nature of online crimes.

Whilst it would be assumed that more computer-mediated contact with clients or potential clients would add safety to sex work given the physical distance, capacities for anonymity and various digital safety tips Beyond the Gaze has uncovered, there are new risks related to the digital environment. Whilst technology-mediated indirect workers (such as webcammers) were much less likely to experience violence at work, they experienced similar levels of harassment and unwanted contact through email, text and social media. Digital risks include: (1) potential victim of harassment, stalking and persistent unwanted behaviour through phone or computer-mediated communication; (2) security online in terms of exposure of profile, personal information, outing and threats to privacy; (3) commercial vulnerability in terms of profiles being deleted, or temporarily turned off by platforms, rendering business precarious and fragile; (4) economically instability due to the changing nature of policing, the potential for platforms to be immediately closed and scrapped by national policing interventions or platform managers changing forum rules/functions/payment system which impact on sex workers, and the long-term threat from possible changes to legislation such as making it a crime to pay for sex.

Operating Beyond the Legislative Gaze?

The legal context of sex work has changed because of the online presence despite the absence of law catching up with the online sex work revolution. Currently amidst the police, law enforcement and protective state organisations, there is limited awareness of online sex markets as police continue to focus on street and managed indoor sectors (Feis-Bryce 2018). Regulation in the UK and recent policy documents fail to pay attention to online markets—not only direct sex workers advertising online, but also newer forms of indirect commercial sexual exchanges which only occur online. While there has been a move from enforcement to safeguarding, the primary focus of policy and policing is on protecting 'victims', modern slavery and child sexual commercial exploitation not considering diversity of online markets, problems relating to rights and safety of independent sex workers or those who are working of their own volition. This also includes migrant workers, who appear to be targeted in operations against so called 'pop-up brothels', and have recently been subjected to media exposure and immediate deportation in what seem like staged police raids to demonstrate something is being done about undocumented workers.[1]

In the interviews with police at strategic and operational levels across all four home nations, (covering 16 forces), monitoring of online activities appeared variable and there was a spectrum of good to bad practice in relation to interaction with online advertising. It appears police do not always understand the data protection and other legal protocols which govern platforms' ability to share data and their need to protect the identity of customers working within the law. While there is no clear consensus on the appropriate regulatory framework for online sex markets, there is general agreement amongst police interviewees that sex workers' safety and protection should be paramount. Yet on the ground, the reality of policing demonstrates that National Police Chief Council (2016) guidelines are not adhered to by many forces as enforcement practices often dominate investigations at the detriment of local multi-agency partnership involvement. Discussion in the fieldwork concluded around the need for a more strategic approach to sex work which does not penalise sex workers or involve activities which make it a more hidden and hard-to-reach industry. If the current trend whereby sex workers do not report to the police crimes experienced in their work is to be changed, the approach of the police needs to be clearly differentiated between enforcement and protection, relying more heavily on detailed intelligence to police organised crime and violations such as trafficking, rather than voluntary sex workers.

Sex Worker Spaces, Peer Support, Activism and Advocacy

We know the Internet has also become an important means of connecting independent sex workers, many of whom have not previously had access to mechanisms for information sharing and mutual support (Ray 2007). We know already, in common with other marginalised groups, sex workers have formed 'virtual' communities (Ashford 2009) alongside customers who gather online to exchange information (Sanders 2008).

Beyond the Gaze has found that the opportunities created by online spaces, which traverse geographic and social boundaries and provide anonymised communication where needed, have enabled sex workers to interact in ways that were difficult before (unless physically working together) and which also may render them subject to legal sanction. Sex workers are very active on a range of different forums—some linked to the larger platforms, others through social media. Online alerts are used for support and safety and workers, projects and organisations such as National Ugly Mugs flag up potentially dangerous individuals to avoid. Peer-led support forums have developed in recent years, with sex workers taking the initiative in developing their own closed spaces to provide practical information and advice, safety being a common concern. These spaces are specifically welcoming of new sex workers who want to learn the tricks of the trade, with more experienced workers revealing important business and safety tips. Described aptly by one sex worker as the 'online water cooler', these digital spaces provide crucial gathering opportunities for colleagues who are often isolated, without the everyday contact to others working in the online sector in their physical work environments, but instead rely on online spaces for immediate advice, communication around safety and to be part of a community.

There is evidence that digital spaces have provided a more fluid and active means of political engagement for sex workers, many of whom do not want to reveal their own identity and can benefit for the anonymous nature of online communication yet still have their say and support others. Activism is alive through online sex worker spaces, where there is resistance, advocacy and momentum to provide a platform for the voices of sex workers. Nonetheless, it is likely that more affluent and middle-class sex workers are using the technology for activities such as blogging and self-expression; although as Ray (2007) has observed, a minority of street worker activists also contribute their views online.

The Digital Future?

These key messages from Beyond the Gaze are filtered through the academic lens and are just a taster of the strong, eloquent and open voices of the 62 sex workers who were interviewed and the 641 respondents who wrote immense amounts of text to explain their experiences. Our project has begun to expose some of the complex dynamics that the digital technologies have created for the sex industries, shining a light on how new opportunities provide increased safety strategies, but at the same time there are new dangers of harassment, surveillance and concerns and worries about becoming a victim of crime or privacy breaches. We are also aware that as we write this book in 2017, developments will already be underway which morph and change the way the online sex industry operates, stemming both from internal technology features to other statutory changes in policing, methods of regulation and even perhaps legal changes. Therefore, the digital sex markets are always in a state of flux, responding to the market, influenced by the political landscape and exploited by those intent on causing harm as well as by the ingenuity and creativeness of the 'tech savvy' sex workers who create new business spaces and opportunities within the shifting online terrain. As greater global uncertainties unfold, mobility of people increases, the gaps between rich and poor widens, and the fluidity of sexualities find spaces for expression, the sex industry will wax and wane in tandem. The online commercial sex revolution provides opportunities for work, empowerment, flexibility and freedom for some, but equally the concerns over precarity of employment, criminalisation, exploitation and lack of protection if sex workers become victims of crime. Current laws and continued structurally embedded stigmatisation of sex work means that many online sex workers remain invisible behind the screen, denied access to full labour rights, full citizenship and access to social justice, pushed increasingly by current laws to work behind the screen.

Note

1. http://www.thisiswiltshire.co.uk/news/15382932.Romanian_sex_workers_to_be_deported_following_immigration_offences/ (Accessed 19th July 2017).
   http://www.independent.co.uk/news/uk/home-news/what-is-it-like-to-be-a-prostitute-sex-worker-laws-uk-police-decriminalisation-a7141636.html (Accessed 19th July 2017).

References

Ashford, C. 2009. Male sex work and the Internet effect: Time to re-evaluate the criminal law? *Journal of Criminal Law* 73 (3): 258–280.

Brennan, D. 2004. *What's love got to do with it? Transnational desires and sex tourism in the Dominican Republic.* Durham: Duke University Press.

Brents, B.G., C.A. Jackson, and K. Hausbeck. 2010. *The state of sex: Tourism, sex, and sin in the new American heartland.* New York: Routledge.

Brewis, J., and S. Linstead. 2000. *Sex, work and sex work: Eroticizing organization.* London: Routledge.

Cunningham, S., and T.D. Kendall. 2011. Prostitution 2.0: The changing face of sex work. *Journal of Urban Economics* 69 (3): 273–287.

Feis-Bryce, A. 2018. Policing sex work in Britain: A patchwork approach. In *Policing the sex industry*, ed. T. Sanders and M. Laing. London: Routledge.

Jones, A. 2015. Sex work in a digital era. *Sociology Compass* 9 (7): 558–570.

NPCC. 2016. *National policing sex work guidance.* London: National Police Chiefs Council.

Peppet, S.R. 2013. Prostitution 3.0? *Iowa Law Review* 98: 1989–2060.

Pitcher, J. 2015. Sex work and modes of self-employment in the informal economy: Diverse business practices and constraints to effective working. *Social Policy and Society* 14 (1): 113–123.

Ray, A. 2007. *Naked on the Internet: Hook-ups, downloads and cashing in on Internet sexploration.* Emeryville: Seal Press.

Sanders, T. 2001. Female street sex workers, sexual violence and protection strategies. *The Journal of Sexual Aggression* 7 (1): 5–18.

Sanders, T. 2005. It's just acting: Sex workers strategies for capitalising on sexuality. *Gender, Work and Organization* 14 (4): 319–342.

Sanders, T. 2008. *Paying for pleasure: Men who buy sex.* Cullompton: Willan.

Sanders, T., L. Connelly, and L. Jarvis-King. 2016. On our own terms: The working conditions of internet-based sex workers in the UK. *Sociological Research Online* 21 (4): 15.

Smith, E.M. 2017. It gets very intimate for me: Discursive boundaries of pleasure and performance in sex work. *Sexualities* 20 (3): 344–363.

Wolkowitz, C., R.L. Cohen, T. Sanders, and K. Hardy (eds.). 2013. *Body/sex/work: Intimate, embodied and sexualized labour.* Basingstoke: Palgrave Macmillan.

Appendix: Data Sample Overview

Sex Worker Interviews: Basic Demographics

- 68% of interviewees were female, 26% male and 6% transgender, 61% identified as straight, 18% as gay or lesbian and 21% as bisexual/bi-curious.
- 71% were White British, 2% White Irish, 8% White European, 6% White other 2% Black, 6% mixed ethnicity and 5% other. 6% of interview participants were migrants.
- For 63% sex work was there only job but for just over a third 37% combined sex work with other work or study.
- The minimum number of hours worked per week in sex work was 2 with a maximum of 60 and most people working between 20–40 hours.

Further information about the socio demographics and key job characteristics of the interview sample is presented in the following tables.

Gender

CIS female	CIS male	Trans	Total no.
42 (68%)	16 (26%)	N = 4 (6%)	62

Appendix: Data Sample Overview

Sexuality

Straight	Gay/lesbian	Bisexual/bi-curious	Total
38 (61%)	11 (18%)	13 (21%)	N = 62

Ethnicity

Ethnicity	No.	%
White British (inc English, Scottish, Welsh)	44	71
White Irish	1	2
White E European	5	8
White other	4	6
Black	1	2
Mixed ethnicity	4	6
Other ethnicity	3	5
Total	62	100

Number migrant workers: 10 (7 female, 2 male, 1 trans)

Qualifications

Qualification level	Female	Male	Trans	Total no.	%
Higher/postgrad degree, level 5	9	3	1	12	
First degree, vocational level 4	10	4	1	15	
Diploma/professional qualifications	3	2	2	7	
A levels, vocational level 3	9	3		12	
GCSE/O Level grade A*-C, level 2	9	3		12	
Qualifications level 1 and below		1		1	
Other qualifications: level unknown	1		1	2	
No qualifications	1			1	

Geographical location

North East	5
North West	12
Yorkshire and Humber	7
South East	5
South West	2
Greater London	10
Eastern Region	3
West Midlands	7
East Midlands	1

Wales	3
Scotland	6
N Ireland	1

Support dependents: 20 (18 female, 2 male)

Current work (some people do more than one)

Current work	Female	Male	Trans	Total
Independent	31	13	4	48
Massage	5	7	1	13
BDSM	11	5	2	18
Cam	15	5	1	21
Other (inc brothel and agency)	17	4	1	22

Main job:

- Independent: 35 (25 female, 6 male, 4 trans)
- Independent with massage or domination: 3 (1 female, 2 male)
- Cam: 6 (5 female, 1 male)
- Combination cam with other work (independent, BDSM): 8 (6 female, 2 male)
- BDSM: 6 (3 female, 3 male)
- Massage: 3 (1 female, 2 male)
- Other: 1 female

Years working as sex worker

Years	No.	%
<1 yr	1	2
1–5 yrs	28	46
6–10 yrs	16	26
11–20 yrs	9	15
More than 20 years	7	11

Always worked same sector: n = 37. 60% had always worked the same sector.

Sectors previously worked in (25):

Street	7
Brothel	10
Adult film	5
Massage	2
Cam	3
Ind/agency	9
Other	2

N.b. Street 3 female, 3 male, 1 trans; brothel 7 female, 3 male.

Sex work only job?

Yes	No
N = 39 (63%)	23 (37%)

Other jobs/activities include (n.b. some more than one):

Student	6
Education/HE teaching	2
Vol sector	4
Training/campaigning	2
Health/social care	5
Therapies/massage	3
Writing/publishing	2
Accountancy	1
Admin/clerical	4
Hotels/catering/services	3
IT	2
Manual work	1
Other sectors various	5

Hours worked per week on sex work:

Min 2, max 60 (most between 20–40 hours).

Number hours	Responses
1–5	1
6–10	3
11–20	19
21–30	14
31–40	9
More than 40	10

Breakdown of tasks:

Client time/hours p.w.	Responses
1–5	8
6–10	17
11–20	18
21–30	3
31–40	0
More than 40	2

Other business-related activities vary between 1–55 hours per week.

Average number clients per week:
Escorting/independent sex work: 0–30 (most frequent 1–10)
Camming: 10–15 regulars, 40–100+ one-offs.

Client gender
Mainly male (61 specified)
10 also have some female, although often rarely
23 also have couples (mainly m/f, but also male only)

Average earnings
Escorting varies from less than £500 to more than £4000 monthly (8 £500–1999, 7 £2000–3999, 9 £4000 and above)
Camming also varies from less than £500 to more than £4000 monthly (5 £500–1999, 1 £2000–3999, 1 £4000 and above, so mainly less than £2000 per month)
Annual—less information here:
Escorting varies from £5000 to more than £60,000 annually (mainly between £10,000 and £49,999)
Cammers didn't give annual earnings.

Working with others:
Most work alone (45)
14 work with other sex workers
Pus 1 receptionist/admin, 1 admin and 1 other.

Sex Worker Survey: About the Respondents

Nearly three-quarters of survey respondents were female, 19% male, 3% transgender and a further 3% non-binary or intersex. A small number of 'others' included those who defined themselves as gender fluid and respondents who only worked as part of a couple, therefore classed themselves as male/female. Three participants did not give their gender.

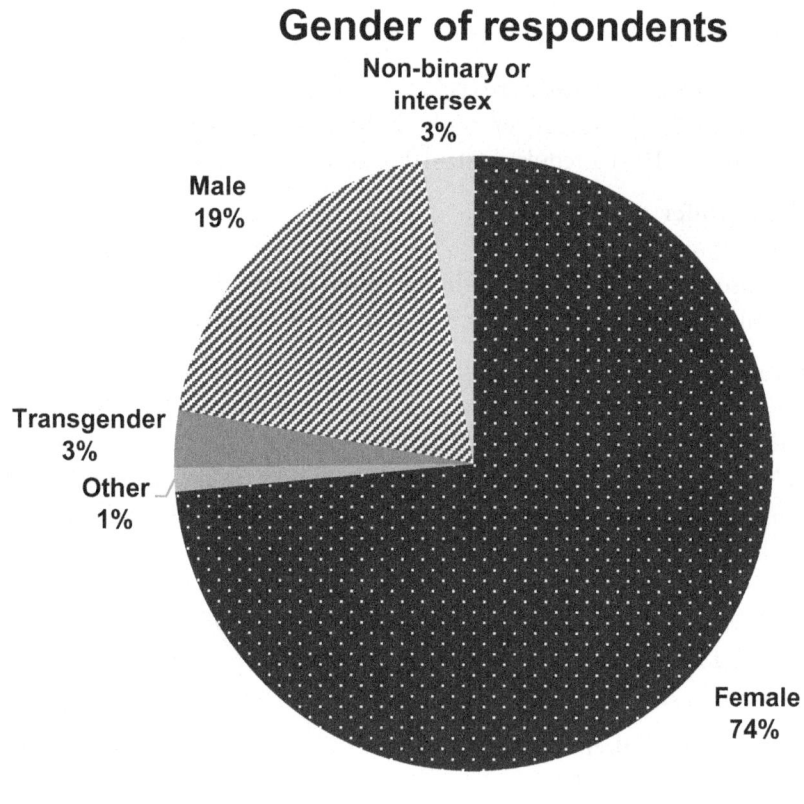

Gender of respondents
- Non-binary or intersex 3%
- Male 19%
- Transgender 3%
- Other 1%
- Female 74%

N=638

The largest group of respondents described themselves as bisexual, with nearly as many classing themselves as straight/heterosexual.

Appendix: Data Sample Overview

How would you describe your sexual orientation?

	No	%
Lesbian	4	0.6
Gay	83	12.9
Straight/heterosexual	249	38.8
Bisexual	268	41.8
Prefer not say	6	0.9
Other	26	4.1
System missing	5	0.8
Total	641	100.0

There was some difference by gender. While 51% of female survey respondents gave their sexuality as straight/heterosexual and 45% as bisexual, only a very small number identified as lesbian. In comparison, 64% of males identified as gay, 28% as bisexual and only 6% as heterosexual.

There was considerable diversity in age, with more than 60% of survey respondents being aged between 25 and 44 at the time of the survey. Similar to other research studies of indoor sex workers, of those who stated their age when starting sex working, many entered in their 20s or 30s. Only 6% started sex working when they were aged under 18 and 5% were aged 45 and above.

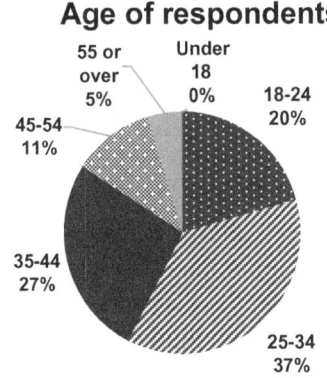

Age of respondents
N=639

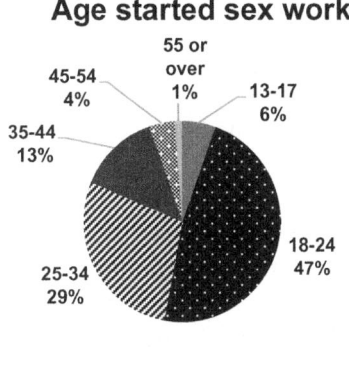

Age started sex work
N=593

The majority of respondents were white, with 73% categorising themselves as White UK. The broad White category also included Irish and East and West European respondents.

Ethnic group

Broad ethnic group	No	%
White	559	87.2
Mixed	32	5.0
Asian/Asian British	17	2.7
Black/Black British	17	2.7
Other	12	1.9
System missing	4	0.6
Total	641	100.0

While the majority of respondents identified their nationality as British, other nationalities included Romanian, Polish, Portuguese and a range of nationalities from Europe and the rest of the world.

Less than half of respondents described themselves as single, with 45% having a partner or cohabiting.

How would you describe your relationship status?

Status	No	%
Single	302	47.1
Cohabiting	104	16.2
Married/civil partnership	105	16.4
Partner don't live with	80	12.5
Prefer not say	29	4.5
Other	16	2.5
System missing	5	0.8
Total	641	100.0

Of those who gave their qualifications, survey respondents were comparatively highly qualified (37% were educated to degree level or higher; a further third possessing qualifications to A level or diploma level). There was no significant difference between males and females.

Appendix: Data Sample Overview

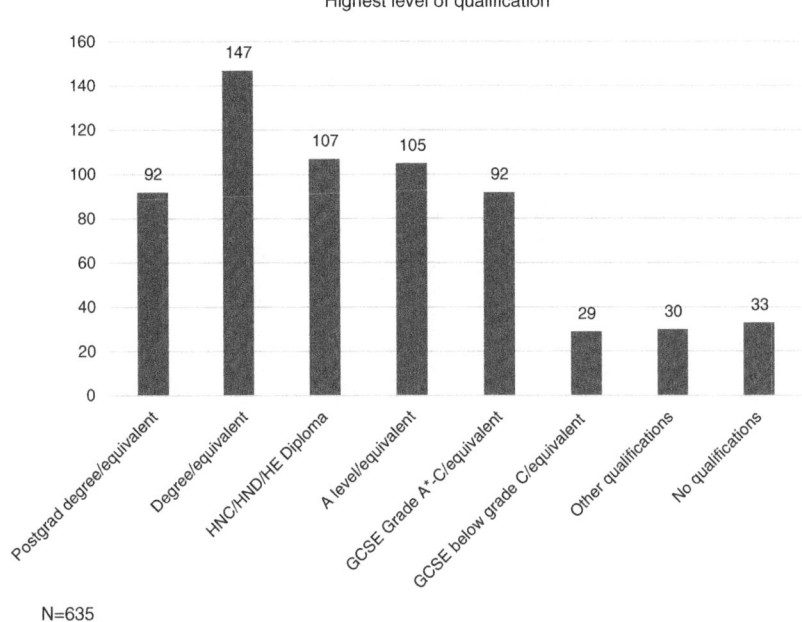

N=635

The majority of respondents (71% out of 636 who responded to this question) did not have any financial dependants. The response to this question differed by gender (two-thirds of females and 89% of males did not have any dependants).

Survey respondents were based across the UK, with the highest proportions being in London, the South East and the North West. A small number of respondents lived outside the UK some of the time and visited periodically for work. While nearly 20% of respondents were based in London and 14% in the South East, 38% indicated that they worked in Greater London and a quarter in the South East, among other locations. As can be seen from the chart below, some people work in more than one geographical area. While sex workers travelled from across the UK to Greater London, there was a degree of mobility between regions, for example, across the North East, North West and Yorkshire and the Humber.

Appendix: Data Sample Overview

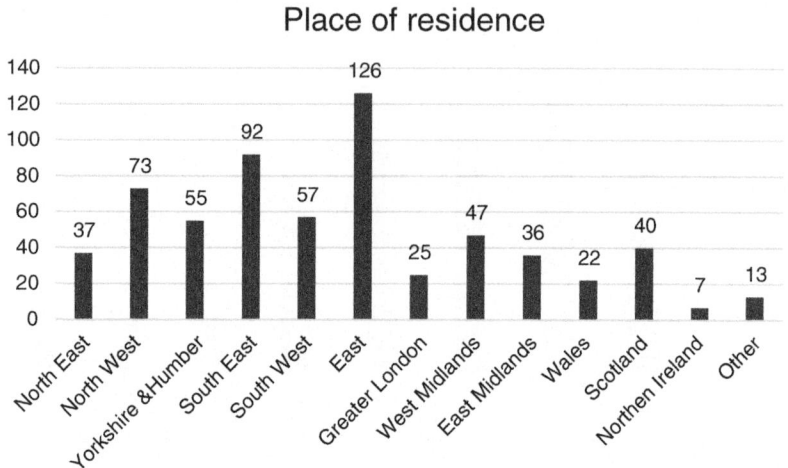

N=630

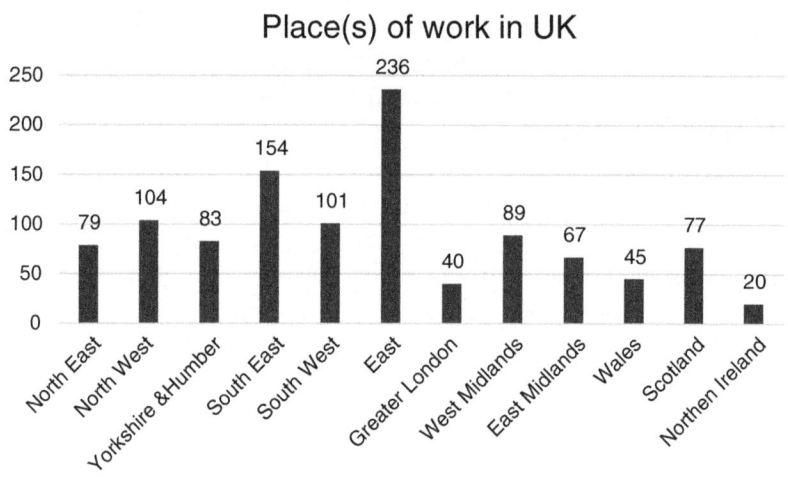

N=641. Multiple response, so percentages add up to more than 100

The majority of respondents (615) worked in independent indoor sectors, categorised as independent sex workers/escorts, webcammers, providers of sexual massage or BDSM services. Respondents often worked in more than one sector in the sex industry. Nearly three-fifths of independent sex workers/escorts undertook some other form of sex work: particularly BDSM (28%), webcamming (27%) and phone sex work (23%). There was a substantial overlap between webcam and phone workers, with nearly 60% of webcam workers also undertaking phone sex work. Half also worked in independent sex work/escorting.

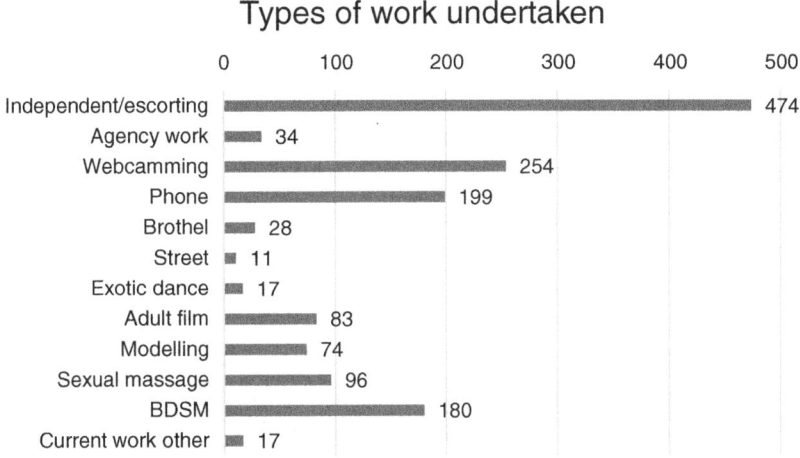

Types of work undertaken

- Independent/escorting: 474
- Agency work: 34
- Webcamming: 254
- Phone: 199
- Brothel: 28
- Street: 11
- Exotic dance: 17
- Adult film: 83
- Modelling: 74
- Sexual massage: 96
- BDSM: 180
- Current work other: 17

N=641. Note: multiple response so percentages add up to more than 100

There was some difference according to gender: for example, while the majority of respondents of all genders worked in independent sex work/escorting, a higher proportion of women than men worked in webcamming, whereas the reverse was true of sexual massage. A small number of both men and women were involved in street work.

The greater proportion of respondents (more than two-thirds) had been doing their current sex work job for 5 years or less. A slightly higher proportion of females than males had been working for more than 5 years.

Index

A

Activism 24, 45–47, 154, 155, 161, 162
Advertising 3, 4, 8–10, 16–18, 25, 26, 29–35, 37–41, 47–50, 57, 58, 61, 64, 77, 78, 81, 97, 100, 103, 104, 123, 127, 130, 131, 133, 135, 136, 138, 140–144, 146–148, 154–156, 160, 161
Apps 9, 16, 31, 32, 39, 100

B

BDSM 7, 15, 17, 27–29, 35, 37, 39, 43, 44, 49, 61–63, 66–69, 73, 74, 77–80, 82, 97, 102, 103, 105, 106, 110, 114, 149, 156
Blogging 46, 162
Buddying systems 106

C

Collaboration 5, 45
Crime
　doxing 5, 157, 159
　harassment 5, 90, 94, 139, 163
　hate crime 130
　misuse of information 157, 159
　stalking 94, 139
Criminalisation 93, 146, 149, 163
Crowd funding 46, 47
Customer forums 34, 36, 103, 154

D

Digitally enabled crime 93
Digital space 4, 162
Digital technology 40, 45, 47, 95, 113, 122, 123, 156, 159
Direct sex work 25, 62

Index

Diversity 24, 29, 43, 48, 56, 59, 67, 78, 81, 124, 125, 128, 148, 158, 160
Doxing 5, 94, 110, 129, 157

E

Earnings 27, 29, 38, 70–74, 81, 157
Escort 3, 4, 16–18, 25, 26, 29–35, 38, 45, 49, 61–65, 67, 69, 73, 74, 77–80, 82, 94, 104, 105, 109–111, 113, 114, 127, 128, 141, 145, 154
Exploitation 10, 69, 123, 124, 128–130, 132, 134–137, 141, 145, 146, 148, 160, 163

F

Facebook 8, 43–46, 49, 94, 96, 101, 102, 104, 109, 143
Facebook groups 44, 102, 104
Facebook messenger 46
Flexibility 62, 67, 70, 131, 156, 163
Fluidity 156, 163

G

Gender 5, 7, 18, 25, 42, 51, 56–59, 62, 66, 81, 82, 90, 108, 125, 154

H

Hacking 75, 97, 109, 144
Human rights 148

I

Independent sex workers 3, 13, 41, 60, 63, 64, 66–68, 71–73, 75, 81, 92, 98, 99, 124, 136, 148, 156, 160, 161
Indirect sex work 2, 15–17, 65, 72, 74, 145
In-person services 2, 15, 36, 158
Instagram 39, 46, 158
Internet 2–6, 10–12, 14–18, 24, 40, 45, 46, 50, 56–67, 70, 72, 74–81, 88, 91, 94–99, 106, 108, 114, 115, 122–128, 131, 132, 134, 135, 138, 140, 146, 148, 149, 158, 159, 161
Internet-based sex work 129
Interviews 5–9, 12, 15, 17, 18, 24, 27, 29, 31, 35, 37, 39, 41, 42, 49, 50, 58, 60, 72, 95, 103, 105, 106, 108, 111, 113, 125, 126, 129, 132, 133, 135, 140, 149, 156, 161
IP address 100, 112

J

Job satisfaction 7, 74, 75

L

Labour processes 157, 158
Labour rights 145, 163
Law 42, 46, 49, 69, 80, 95, 100, 107, 122–125, 131, 132, 135, 141, 142, 144, 146, 148, 160, 161
Limitations to study 10

Index

M

Mainstream jobs 3
Marketing 3, 9, 12, 27, 31, 35–37, 39–41, 43, 47, 49, 50, 64, 69, 75, 77–79, 81, 154
Messaging apps 43
Methods 6, 8, 38, 91, 93, 97, 98, 100, 108, 112, 114–116, 156, 159, 163
Migrant sex work 3, 7, 10, 11, 56, 60, 61, 64, 81, 108
Mobile phone 136
Mobile phone technology 106
Modern slavery 10, 11, 64, 81, 124–126, 130, 132, 134, 136, 138, 160
Motivations 37, 47

N

National Ugly Mugs 12, 101, 102, 127, 140, 141, 162

O

Online harassment 90
Online platforms 40, 46, 103, 122, 125, 131, 140–142, 144, 147, 149, 159
Online privacy 5, 70, 88, 109, 111
Online sex work 14, 17, 24, 29, 47–49, 65, 81, 123, 126, 131, 132, 134, 149, 154, 157, 159, 160
Online spaces 10, 12, 24, 41, 45, 47, 50, 88, 103, 112, 154, 162
Online stalking 110
Outing 94, 110, 115, 160

P

Partnerships 5, 12
Peer support 39, 40, 43, 44, 161
Persistent or repeated unwanted contact or attempts to contact 89, 90, 115
Platforms 4, 9, 10, 13, 15, 16, 24–27, 29, 31, 33–35, 38, 39, 41, 43–50, 100, 101, 103–105, 109, 114, 127, 129, 130, 132, 135, 139–141, 143, 145, 147, 148, 154–156, 160–162
Policing 5, 14, 122, 123, 125, 126, 129, 130, 133, 135, 144, 148, 149, 160, 161, 163
Policy 6, 11, 13, 32, 34, 45, 56, 95, 123–126, 129, 132, 135–137, 140, 148, 149, 160
Postmodern sex work 158
Privacy 5, 7, 33, 39, 43, 70, 88, 93, 109, 111–115, 129, 138, 157, 159, 160, 163
Prostitution 4, 12, 13, 123, 124, 129, 136, 149

R

Regulation 5, 7, 122, 123, 130, 131, 143, 145–148, 160, 163
Reporting crime 93, 95

S

Safeguarding 130, 132, 134, 136, 140, 142, 148, 149, 160
Safety strategies
 deterrents 115
 protection 98
 screening 97, 98, 159

Screening 37, 77, 96–100, 103, 104, 106, 159
Sex markets 3, 4, 10, 24, 49, 123, 126, 135, 148, 149, 155, 157, 160, 161, 163
Sex work advocacy 40, 45, 47, 161, 162
Sex worker 7, 8, 10–12, 14–16, 18, 25, 27, 28, 30, 32–41, 43–50, 56, 61–65, 67, 69, 72, 74, 77–80, 92, 95–97, 100–108, 114, 128, 133, 134, 136, 138, 140, 154, 155, 159, 161, 162
Sex worker activism 45, 46
Sex worker forum 44
Sex worker involvement 14
Sex worker rights 45–47
SMS 15, 106, 154
Snap chat 16, 39
Social media 3, 8, 9, 13, 38–40, 43–47, 79, 89, 90, 100, 103, 106, 109, 113–115, 155, 157, 159, 160, 162
Stigma 47, 99, 111, 128, 145, 157
Students 60, 128, 156
Survey 5–8, 10–13, 17, 24, 29, 36, 37, 40, 42, 43, 48–50, 56–63, 66, 67, 69, 70, 72, 75, 82, 88, 90–92, 95–98, 100, 103, 105–108, 111, 113, 115, 138, 144, 145, 149, 156

T

Technology-mediated sex work 159
Timewaster 37, 50, 101, 103

Trafficking 10, 11, 64, 81, 123–126, 130, 132–136, 141, 143–145, 147, 148, 161
Travel to work/touring 63, 65, 81, 136, 156
Tumblr 46
Twitter 8, 9, 29, 39, 40, 43–46, 79, 102, 106, 109

U

Ugly Mugs 97, 100–102, 104, 143

V

Verbal abuse 89, 90, 92, 115
Virtual Private Network 112
Vlogging 46, 158
Vulnerability 124, 126, 128, 132, 134–137, 148, 160

W

Webcammer 16, 18, 44, 94, 96, 97, 109, 145
Webcamming 4, 7, 15, 17, 18, 27, 29, 30, 37, 44, 62, 66–68, 74, 76, 98, 105, 106, 109, 110, 113, 123, 128, 129, 154, 157
WhatsApp 7, 43, 44, 109
Whorephobic 46
Working conditions 7, 75, 124, 138, 145, 148, 157
Working practices 24, 56, 75, 81, 95, 99, 115, 122, 138, 158